Motivational (

MW00936527

By Sue Burgess

Published by:
Sue Burgess Ministries, Inc.
P.O. Box 2766
Mesa, AZ 85214
www.sueburgess.org

Motivational Gifts- God's Gift to You
(Revised)
Copyright 2014 by Sue Burgess
ISBN- 13:978-1532760341
ISBN-10:1532760345

Scripture taken from the King James Version and the New King James Translation

Other Books by Sue Burgess:

The Fruit of the Spirit

The Completed Work of Calvary- Volume 1

The Completed Work of Calvary- Volume 2

Acknowledgements

I would like to acknowledge the many incredible teachers that have been instrumental in helping to shape this book. Among them is Marilyn Hickey, who first introduced me to the wonderful Motivational Gifts in the Word.

Also, a heartfelt thanks to my precious pastors, the late Robert and Vonetta Watson who lovingly spent many years teaching me how to research the truths in the Bible. They were living examples of how to live a victorious Holy Spirit led life in the Word and I miss them daily.

Motivational Gifts- God's Gift to You

Table of Contents

The Gifts of the Bible

Chapter 1

Every person that is birthed into the earth system is uniquely handcrafted by the Lord for a specific purpose and destiny. Isaiah states that the LORD is the potter Who molds us to His specifications and we are the clay. God tenderly forms each one with great attention to even the smallest detail. We are the personal artwork of the Master Craftsman.

> "But now, O LORD, You are our Father; We are the clay, and You our potter; And all we are the work of Your hand..." Isaiah 64:8

The Word tells us that you are the work of the Father's hands, meaning that at the time He formed you, He placed within you all that you would ever need to live a life of victory and purpose. You are tailor-made to His specifications. He has placed within you very individual talents and gifts. There is no one created like you. You are "one-of-a-kind," and you are programmed for a fulfilling life in the earth and a glorious eternity in Heaven.

Talents

Talents and gifts are not the same. The word "talent" comes from the Greek word "talanton." It is a derivative of "tlao" meaning to bear; a balance; a certain weight. It can also mean a sum of money. It also expresses "to bear" meaning a talent might be a voice to sing; an ability to write; to teach; wisdom in finances; perhaps even an artistic flair; etc. It is important to remember that talents are not who you are. They are an addition to who you are. The amount of the talent or talents has no bearing on your success with the talents. Some have more talents, some have less, however; you are only responsible for the talent or talents that you received from the Lord. The Word admonishes us to be a good steward of the talent as there is coming a day when we will each stand before the Lord for an accounting of what we did with the talents He bestowed upon us.

> "So he who had received five talents came and brought five other talents, saying, 'Lord, you delivered to me five talents; look, I have gained five more talents besides them.' His lord said to him, 'Well done, good and faithful servant; you were faithful over a few things, I will make you ruler over many things. Enter into the joy of your lord.'" Matthew 25:20-21

Note: It is important to read the words of Jesus with the finished work of Calvary in mind. At the time Jesus spoke this parable, he had not yet gone to the cross of Calvary and those he was speaking with were still living under the Old Testament Covenant. Today the believer is not a servant, but a child of God, redeemed by the Blood of Jesus. Each of us, as a son or daughter of the Most High God, will stand before the throne of God and receive rewards for the work we have done in the earth. Each will answer the question of the Lord, "What have you done with what I have given you?"

Gifts of the Holy Spirit

There are three categories of "gifts" in the New Testament. The category that most commonly comes to mind is the "gifts of the Holy Spirit" that are listed in 1 Corinthians 12. The gifts of the Holy Spirit are unique in that they never belong to the believer. The Holy Spirit always retains ownership. A more accurate description of the gifts of the Holy Spirit would be "manifestations" of the Holy Spirit. These gifts are always at the unction of the Holy Spirit Himself and never function at the will of man.

According to Vines Expository, the Greek word used here for "gifts" is "charisma." In this scripture, it speaks of "His endowment upon believers by the operation of the Holy Spirit in the churches." This is not only for "five-fold" ministers. Any believer that is baptized with the Holy Ghost is qualified to operate in the manifestations of the Spirit as the Holy Spirit wills.

> "But the manifestation of the Spirit is given to each one for the profit of all: for to one is given the word of wisdom through the Spirit, to another the word of knowledge through the same Spirit, to another faith by the same Spirit, to another gifts of healings by the same Spirit, to another the working of miracles, to another prophecy, to another discerning of spirits, to another different kinds of tongues, to another the interpretation of tongues." 1 Corinthians 12:7-10

The manifestations of the Spirit are divided into three categories. They are:

Revelation gifts: These gifts "reveal" something.

- **The Word of Knowledge**- this gift manifests as just a word, or a thought that supernaturally reveals something of the past or present.

- **The Word of Wisdom**- much like the word of knowledge, but this word or thought supernaturally reveals a future event.

- **The Discerning of Spirits**- the ability to "see;" to "perceive" into the spirit realm. Most of those that operate in this gift "see" into both the demonic and the heavenly angelic realm. God has placed limitations on this manifestation. The discerning of spirits does not "see" into or "perceive" **the mind of man,** as that is in the natural realm. This is not the "gift of suspicion." Some have mistakenly believed that through the operation of this gift, they could "read" the thoughts of other people. Only God knows the heart of man and God is not a gossip. The devil never knows what a man or woman is thinking until they reveal it through their speech.

Power gifts: These gifts "do" something.

- **The Gift of Faith**- the supernatural faith of God hooks up where your faith leaves off and puts you over into victory.

- **The Gifts of Healing**- This is the only gift that is plural. Miraculous healings of all kinds are evident with this gift.

- **The Working of Miracles**- This gift is miraculous and defies all natural explanation. A leg grows out;

tumors disappear; the dead are raised are just three examples that would be classified the working of miracles.

Utterance gifts: These gifts "say" something.

- **Tongues**- this gift is twofold. It may be a message of tongues in your heavenly language bringing forth a divinely inspired message from God. It may also be tongues spoken in a language that is not known to you, but is known to another person in the congregation. One time, as I was praying for a woman at the end of a service, the tongues changed into a language that I had not before experienced. It was quite lengthy. After the service, her daughter came up to me to share what the Lord had done for her mother. Her mother was visiting from South Korea. She had left the way of the Lord several years earlier. The Holy Spirit spoke to her in Korean (her native tongue) revealing private, intimate details of her life that only God could have known. I don't know what He said to her, but the Holy Spirit convicted her heart and called her back into the fold. She repented before the throne of God and renewed her relationship with the Lord. This was very personal between that South Korean woman and the Lord, but God chose to use tongues in a miraculous way to reach her heart.

- **Interpretation of Tongues**- this is when the message in tongues is interpreted so that all in the congregation may have understanding. The scripture admonishes us to pray that when we have a message in tongues that we may also bring forth the interpretation.

"Therefore let him who speaks in a tongue pray that he may interpret." 1 Corinthians 14:13

- Prophecy- this gift brings forth edification, encouragement and exhortation to the Body of Christ. Prophecy may foretell the future and uplifts the congregation.

The gifts or manifestations of the Holy Spirit are used mainly in the congregational services and are purposed to bless the Body of Christ. These gifts usually accompany the office of the evangelist and are a sign to the unbeliever.

The Holy Spirit does not over-ride the free will of man. He only flows through willing vessels. These manifestations operate at the unction of the Holy Spirit coupled with the yielding of the believer. Probably most, if not all, can point to a time when they did not yield to the Spirit, and the Lord did not have His perfect will in a service. There are many reasons for this. Perhaps one was young in the moving of the Holy Spirit and was unsure of what to do; possibly even afraid to speak out. God is merciful and will gently teach us to follow Him. All it takes is a willing heart that is surrendered to the Spirit of God.

There is one last note on the operation of the gifts of the Holy Spirit. Every person in the congregation is to be in submission to the pastor, or the minister that has the service. If what you have in your spirit is the moving of the Holy Spirit of God, God Himself will make room in the service for you to share under the unction of the Holy Spirit. If no room is made, you must be quiet. The Holy Spirit in the Pastor is not in competition with the Holy Spirit in you. There is one Holy Spirit and God is a God of order and not of confusion. The Lord will never call upon you to bring disorder in a church service. Remember, God is not in a hurry and He works all things together in His perfect harmony.

1 Corinthians 12, 13 and 14 are important chapters to study concerning the orderly use of the manifestations of the Holy Spirit in the church.

"Let all things be done decently and in order." 1 Corinthians 14:40

Note: The gifts of the Holy Spirit are really in a category by themselves as He always retains ownership. These gifts reveal the power and character of God, not man. The gifts or manifestations of the Holy Spirit are the work of the Third Person of the Trinity of God on the earth. They are never a part of the believers call or personality; rather they are the faithfulness and love of God in action. He is gracious in that He moves through believers allowing the child of God to be a partner with Him as He manifests the Glory of God on earth.

Hardwired Gifts

However; your motivational gift and the five-fold ministry office gifts are "hardwired" into you at the time God forms you and places you in your mother's womb. They are not "what you do," but are an integral part of the essence of your being.

Many times, spiritual realities are reflected through natural examples. Long before a building is to be constructed, plans are drawn up. These plans consider many factors. The purpose of the building is critical. The design of the building is laid out with the purpose in mind. For example, the amount of electricity that will be needed to fulfill the purpose is "hardwired" into the building at the time of construction.

This is also a spiritual truth. The next two categories of "gifts" are "hardwired" into you by the design of God to enable to fulfill your God given purpose. They make up who you are. It is the unique, individual equipping given by the Lord at the time He forms you and places you in your mother's womb. These gifts and callings cannot be changed. They will always be who you are.

These components make up the essence of your being. You were divinely created by the Master Craftsman for a specific purpose. He has equipped you with all the callings, gifts and talents necessary for you to successfully fulfill that destiny. The Lord has placed within you all that it takes to live a victorious, fruitful, purposeful, blessed and joyful life on this earth.

Fivefold Ministry Office Gifts

"Therefore He says: "When He ascended on high, He led captivity captive, and gave gifts to men." Ephesians 4:8

The Greek word for "gifts" here is "doma," literally meaning "a present."

"And He Himself gave some to be apostles, some prophets, some evangelists, and some pastors and teachers," Ephesians 4:11

Therefore, in this context, the five-fold ministry office gifts (the Apostle, Prophet, Evangelist, Pastor and Teacher) are

God's personal presents or gifts to the Body of Christ (the Church) as a whole.

"For the gifts and calling of God are without repentance." Romans 11:29

Note: The five-fold ministry office gifts are specific gifts of God to the church, however, to the individual; it is a **call** of God on their life. The Apostle, Prophet, Evangelist, Pastor and Teacher are **called** and **ordained** of God to be His gifts to the Body of Christ. The call is their purpose, their God given destiny. God equips them with all that is needed to fulfill that divine purpose.

We have some insight into God's "mode of operation" in Jeremiah. The Word states that the Lord knew, sanctified and ordained Jeremiah **before** He formed him. He placed the call of the Prophet upon Jeremiah before He placed Jeremiah in his mother's womb. The Lord had a purpose, and then He formed Jeremiah with great detail to perfectly fulfill that purpose. That is how the Lord formed and equipped you, with great precision, endowing you with all you need to accomplish your God given purpose and to fulfill His plan for you.

"Before I formed you in the womb I knew you; Before you were born I sanctified you; I ordained you a prophet to the nations." Jeremiah 1:5

The question is: Does God assign a five-fold ministry office calling to every believer?

The answer is: No. Not every believer is called to a five-fold ministry office. The Body of Christ is very diverse. Not all members have the same purpose. However, the Lord lovingly designs each individual member perfectly

9

with everything they need to successfully fulfill their specific purpose. If everyone were given a five-fold ministry office calling, then the church (Body) could be likened to a person that is all hands. That person would be lacking many parts and the end result would be dysfunction.

Remember, the five-fold ministry offices gifts are actually "callings." It is an individual ordination from the Lord for a specific purpose, placed within a person at the time they were created. It is the path God has ordained for them to journey on the earth.

Note: If you have a five-fold ministry call of God on your life **it is a mandate, not a request.** It is your purpose woven into your destiny. An old Scotch saying states it well. "It is the cut of the cloth."

If God has called you into one or more of the five-fold ministry offices, He placed within you that call at the moment of creation. You are "hardwired" for that call. Man cannot call himself. These gifts do not flow from the will of man. The supernatural unction to operate in a ministry office gift comes from the throne of God.

There can be confusion about whether you are called into the five-fold office gifts. Only God can verify your calling to you. It may be an inward witness and then be confirmed by another; it may just be between you and the Lord. If you are called, God will make His plan clear to you.

THE LOCAL CHURCH

God's purpose for the five-fold ministry office gifts is revealed in Ephesians 4:12.

> "For the equipping of the saints for the work of ministry, for the edifying of the body of Christ,"

In his book, "The Ministry Gifts," the late Kenneth Hagin states "If one purpose for which the ministry gifts are given is the perfecting of the saints, will they ever reach maturity without them?" The answer is "No." You will never reach the full stature of the gift within you without faithfully sitting under the five-fold ministry gifts that God so graciously placed within the local church to bless the Body of Christ.

The Lord set up the local church body to perfect or mature you for the work of the ministry and for the edifying of the Body of Christ. The destiny given to you will never come to fruition until you are obedient to Hebrews 10:25 and become an integral part of a local body of believers. It is in the local church that your call and gifts will become active and grow. No one is ever so gifted that they can fulfill God's plan and purpose without a local church body. God operates within order and unity. We need each other. None are called by the Lord to be "Lone Rangers," EVER.

> "Not forsaking the assembling of ourselves together, as is the manner of some, but exhorting one another, and so much the more as you see the Day approaching." Hebrews 10:25

God will not set you forth in ministry until you have had time to mature and settle. God does not set the novice forth, but He thoroughly prepares and equips you for the task He has given you. The calling of God will be evident on your life. He supernaturally gifts you for the purpose He has for you. You will never have to announce your call. The call announces you!

11

Note: Not every person created is called into the five-fold ministry office gifts, but literally each and every person has been given a motivational gift.

An often used illustration of the five-fold ministry office gifts compares these gifts to the five fingers of the hand.

OFFICE OF APOSTLE

The thumb could be representative of the Apostle as it is the thumb that inter-works with the whole hand. The apostle's office calling impacts all other ministry office callings. An apostle is a "sent one." He goes forth, preaches, teaches, establishes churches, and then usually goes on to do the same thing again in another place. Paul is the greatest apostle that ever lived. "Missionary" might be a modern day term for apostle. Apostles normally function in all five of the ministry office gifts.

The five-fold ministry office gifts and the motivational gifts often seem to meld together. However; they are distinctly separate.

Paul stood in the office gift of apostle, but he was also a motivational gift of teaching. We can identify his motivational gift by the earmarks of his personality. He was an intense researcher even before he had an encounter with Jesus and became a believer. His knowledge of the Law was legendary. He studied under some of the best teachers of the day. He was a Roman citizen, and was adept in Roman law as well as Hebrew law. After he received Jesus as his Savior, he studied the cultures of the Gentiles so that he could "be all things to all people that he could by any means save some." Everything about Paul reveals he was called to be an apostle and he was a motivational gift of teaching.

Even if you are called and ordained of God to the office of Apostle or any other office gift, you are still endowed with a specific motivational gift.

OFFICE OF PROPHET

The Prophet is the forefinger and he points the way. In searching the scriptures you will find that there are three main functions of the office of Prophet: teacher, seer and the mouthpiece of God.

True prophets also stand in the office of teacher. The teaching anointing is clearly evident in their ministry. The prophet also speaks the oracles of God through divine inspiration. He is a "seer," a "perceiver" and through the anointing of the Holy Spirit is able to discern the motives and intents of the heart. The prophet confronts sin wherever sin is found.

The prophet encourages, uplifts and edifies the Body of Christ as well as shares forthcoming moves of the Lord. The Lord never sets the prophet forth until he has matured in the Word of God. It is not for the baby believer. God seasons, equips, tempers and tests before He ever sets the prophet out. Prophets usually operates in all of the gifts of the Spirit. A prophet always functions in at least the Word of Knowledge, the Word of Wisdom, Prophecy and the Discerning of Spirits.

Jeremiah is listed as a prophet in the Old Testament. His life revealed that he was also a motivational gift of mercy.

He agonized over the plight of the people of Israel. He was labeled the "weeping prophet."

Elijah is also an Old Testament prophet. However, his ministry revealed he was most likely a motivational gift of prophecy. He saw only "black or white" concerning sin, showed little mercy, was fierce in his confrontation of sin and openly and publicly challenged the prophets of Baal.

We have prophets in the earth today. The late Kenneth Hagin stood in the office of prophet. Kenneth Copeland also stands in that office, and he prophesied under the unction of the Holy Ghost that "the Berlin Wall would fall in one day." It was only three months later that it fell "in one day."

OFFICE OF EVANGELIST

The evangelist could be represented by the middle finger. The heart of the evangelist burns for souls to be saved as they beckon unbelievers to the Cross of Calvary while passionately proclaiming the gospel of Jesus Christ. They usually generate great excitement among the people as they operate freely in the gifts of the Holy Spirit, and the Lord works with them confirming His Word with signs following. They are "traveling preachers" continually moving throughout the earth preaching and teaching the completed work of Calvary.

Philip is an example of a New Testament evangelist and signs and wonders accompanied his ministry.

"And the next day we that were of Paul's company departed, and came unto Caesarea: and we entered into the house of Philip the evangelist, which was one of the seven; and abode with him." Acts 21:8

"And the people with one accord gave heed unto those things which Philip spoke, hearing and seeing the miracles which he did." Acts 8:6

Philip was also a motivational gift of serving. Acts 6 gives an account of how he was one of seven men chosen to serve tables and to care for the widows of Israel.

T. L. Osborn is an evangelist in the earth today. In his meetings it is common for the deaf to hear, the dumb to speak, blind eyes to open and see clearly, cripples walk and leap for joy and the awesome wonders of the Lord are revealed to the masses. Only God knows how many millions have been saved through his stewardship of the evangelistic call of God on his life.

Billy Graham is another well-known example of an evangelist. Throngs throughout the world have come to know Jesus as their personal Lord and Savior through the work of his ministry.

OFFICE OF PASTOR

The pastor could best be represented by the ring finger as he is "married" to the flock. The pastor carries the people in his heart. He tenderly nurtures the lambs. Pastors have a steady, abiding love for the people God has entrusted to them. They are responsible to feed their flock, protect their flock, and care for the needs of their flock. Pastors preach, teach and lead their flock into maturity. As shepherds of their flocks, the responsibility of the church rests upon their shoulders. The manifestation gifts of the Holy Spirit usually accompany the office of pastor. The pastor is accountable before the Lord for the lambs God has entrusted to his care.

Jesus is our example of a shepherd or pastor. He willingly laid down His life for His sheep.

"I am the good shepherd, and know my sheep, and am known of mine." John 10:14

OFFICE OF TEACHER

The office gift of teacher could be represented by the little finger, as they bring a balance to the hand. When one stands in the office of teacher, they teach the Word by divine revelation of God. They study the Word, but it is the supernatural ability of the Holy Ghost and His anointing upon them that enables them to bring forth the teaching gift. They are able to take the principles of God revealed in the Word; break them down into bite sized pieces and feed them to the flock in a way that is easily digested. They help the pastor to grow the flock into maturity.

Paul stood both in the office of Apostle and Teacher. He not only was called and ordained to the office of teacher, but he was also a motivational gift of teaching.

"Whereunto I am ordained a preacher, and an apostle, (I speak the truth in Christ, and lie not) a teacher of the Gentiles in faith and verity." 1Timothy 2:7 *KJV*

The late Reverend Charles Capps, Joyce Meyer and Andrew Womack are well known examples of the five-fold ministry office of teacher today.

MOTIVATIONAL GIFTS

Have you ever wondered just where you fit in and just what your personal gifts are? Ever contemplated why you do things the way you do and why you become agitated when others don't seem to care about details the way you do? The answer to these questions and more is found in the study of motivational gifting.

For instance, the one that is a motivational gift of organization becomes very distressed with disorder. Another person takes it in stride. Some people, as in the motivational gift of prophecy, seem stricter than others with less allowance for error. Some in the body are wonderful and pleasant until you are yoked with them in a task. Suddenly they become demanding or bossy. Then there are those that need to be noticed and profusely thanked for their service and there are those that need no attention for the work that they have accomplished. These are all examples of various motivational gifts in the Body trying to work together.

"For as we have many members in one body, and all members have not the same office: So we, being many, are one body in Christ, and every one members one of another. Having then **gifts differing according to the grace that is given to us**, whether prophecy, let us prophesy according to the proportion of faith; Or ministry, let us wait on our ministering: or he that teaches, on teaching; Or he that exhorts, on exhortation: he that gives, let him do it with simplicity; he that rules, with diligence; he that shows mercy, with cheerfulness." Romans 12:4-8

The Greek word used for "gifts' here is also "charisma." Strong's Concordance gives the meaning in this scripture as: "(a (divine) gratuity, i.e. deliverance (from danger or passion); (specifically) a (spiritual) endowment, i.e. (subjectively) religious qualification or (objectively) miraculous faculty :")

Some call these gifts "grace gifts," but the term "motivational gifts" portrays a more accurate picture of the nature of this particular divine equipping. These gifts are the powerful motivating force behind your personality. They are a vital ingredient of the sum total of your being and they guide the direction of your life.

It is important to remember that your motivational gifting alone is not the sum total of the essence of your being. It is a major component; however, it is only one of the ingredients that the Lord places within each person at the time of creation. No two people are created alike. **This study will clarify the most distinctive traits common to each gift.** Keep in mind that within each person, there is a kaleidoscope of nuances that paint the complete portrait of individuality.

There has been much confusion concerning the individual motivational gifting that the Lord places in each person at the moment of creation. This study is specifically designed to enable you to locate and understand what motivational gift you are and where you function best in the Body of Christ. When you are doing what you are designed to do, you become fulfilled in your purpose and destiny. Life takes on a whole new meaning.

There are a multitude of additional benefits you will receive as you prayerfully study the motivational gifts. One is you will discover you do not receive offense as easily as you are now able to identify and understand the personality traits inherent in the different gifts.

As you recognize the gifting and calling that the Lord has created in you, and the gifting that the Lord has placed in others, you will find your capacity for patience is increased. Understanding and identifying motivational gifts help to bring unity and harmony to the Body of Christ.

Also, as each comes to know and appreciate the variety of gifts God Himself has placed in the Body of Christ, the problems created by such emotions as envy and jealousy are eliminated. Recognizing and understanding the gift in others brings the revelation that every child of God possesses his or her own purpose and their individual gifting is part of the Lord's equipping them for the fulfillment of their God given destiny. It is difficult to be jealous or envious of others when you acknowledge the plan and purpose of God working in their lives.

Your motivational gift is easily recognized by very distinctive characteristics that reveal both incredible strengths and inherent weaknesses. Your strengths identify the limitations and boundaries of your gifting; your weaknesses identify potential problem areas. Awareness brings the information you need to more accurately judge what could be a trouble spot for you and therefore, enables you to take steps to compensate for, and to work on, that specific area of your life.

When your motivational gift is known to you, you will find that the purpose and path that the Lord has ordained for your life is clarified.

All born again believers will operate in each of these gifts when necessary, but as you study the motivational gifts, you will find one motivational gift that is primary to you. That motivational gift will be dominant in your personality. For instance, all believers will be kind and merciful to a certain extent, but if you are a motivational gift of mercy, you will consistently display nothing but mercy. Mercy will be one of the most prominent characteristics of your personality and will naturally and consistently flow from your innermost being. Mercy leaps to the forefront of every situation. Mercy will color your vision. When described by another, "gentle, kind, compassionate and loving" are the adjectives that are commonly used.

As you grow in your relationship with the Lord and mature in your spiritual walk, you will find that your motivational gift becomes tempered and balanced. Your confidence will grow as you become more comfortable with the gift you are.

As the five-fold ministry office gifts are "hardwired" at the time of your creation, so are the motivational gifts. These gifts are an integral part of who you are and cannot be changed. They encompass your personality, your viewpoint on life, and your passions. The motivational gift that you are is literally the motivating force behind your decisions and actions.

The seven motivational gifts listed in Romans 12:4-8 that we will be studying in depth are:

- Prophecy
- Server
- Teacher
- Exhorter
- Giver
- Organizer

- Mercy

This study will reveal to you:

- The definition of each gift.

- The function of that gift.

- The particular strengths and weaknesses of each gift.

- Where your gift fits best in the Body of Christ.

- The vocations that flow the easiest with each gift.

- How your particular gifting is central to your life and being.

Motivational Gift of Prophecy

Chapter 2

The motivational gift of prophecy is not to be confused with the Office Gift of the Prophet, or the Holy Spirit's "gift (manifestation) of prophecy." Motivational gifts are a separate category of gifting. The motivational gift of prophecy may, but does not necessarily, stand in the Office of Prophet.

While there are certainly variations of each gift, each motivational gift is easily identified by the set of very distinct characteristics that are inherent within that gifting. I call these traits "earmarks" as they accurately reveal the specific motivational gift type.

The Motivational Gift of Prophecy is Intuitive in Their Perceptions:

This gift is very complex and is difficult to define in a few words. You may be a motivational gift of prophecy. If so, you intuitively "perceive," "discern" and "see" into the intents and the inner heart motives of others under the unction of the Holy Spirit. An earmark of the motivational gift of prophecy is that you possess a natural built-in radar, a keen insight, an intuitive sense about other people as they really are before the Lord.

This particular attribute can be a two edged sword. The ability to discern the truth about others is absolutely inherent within the motivational gift of prophecy, but within that gifting resides tremendous responsibility and great accountability. Not everything that the Lord reveals is intended to be public knowledge. It is one thing to have insight in your spirit and quite another to perceive what to do with the knowledge. Only the Lord can reveal to you what you are to do with the information you receive from the Holy Spirit. There are times when intercession for another is the correct course of action. Perhaps the Lord will send you privately to an individual with a word from Him. Sometimes the Lord will have you publicly share a revelation or a word from God. God may also cause you to warn another of a hidden motive that could cause destruction. It is prudent to remain silent until you are sure what the Lord would have you to do. Always remember it is never right to cause harm in the life of another, and gossip is never sanctioned by our loving God.

Another problem may present itself at times to the motivational gift of prophecy. Because of the prophetic nature of this gift, there may be incidents of others seeking or demanding that you give them a "word' from God. That person is attempting to stand you in the place of God in their life. Never fall prey to this snare of the enemy. If God Himself has not given you a message from His throne, do not be pressured to manufacture something to please another. Allow the integrity of the Lord to guide you and stay true to the motivational gift God placed within you. It is correct to simply say, "The Lord has not revealed anything to me on this." Encourage that person to pray and obtain their own answer from the Lord. The Lord desires a personal relationship with each child and He will always speak to the one that seeks His Face if their ears are open to hear.

The Motivational Gift of Prophecy is an Intense Personality:

John, the Baptist is a classic example of the motivational gift of prophecy. He wore attention getting clothes; ate wild locusts; pointed the finger at sin; and he spoke frankly and persuasively. John, the Baptist even confronted the priests and scribes by calling them vipers and hypocrites and then demanding that they too repent. He added insult to injury when he publicly demanded they produce "fruit of repentance." Essentially, he openly called them sinners and liars. He was fierce and uncompromising. Also, he was not "politically correct" as he publicly called King Herod an adulterer.

> "For John came unto you in the way of righteousness, and ye believed him not: but the publicans and the harlots believed him: and ye, when ye had seen it, repented not afterward, that ye might believe him." Matthew 21:32

> "As it is written in the book of the words of Isaiah the prophet, saying, 'The voice of one crying in the wilderness, Prepare ye the way of the Lord, make his paths straight.' Every valley shall be filled, and every mountain and hill shall be brought low; and the crooked shall be made straight, and the rough ways shall be made smooth; and all flesh shall see the salvation of God. Then said he to the multitude that came forth to be baptized of him, O generation of vipers, who hath warned you to flee from the wrath to come? Bring forth therefore fruits worthy of repentance, and begin not to say within yourselves, we have Abraham to our father: for I say unto you, That God is able of these stones to raise up children unto Abraham." Luke 3:4-8

24

Elijah was also a motivational gift of prophecy. Like John, the Baptist, he openly confronted sin, spoke frankly and persuasively, publicly stood and declared the decrees of God even when faced with personal danger. He made a spectacular display as he ordered water poured on the sacrifice. He also amazed all when he raced Ahab's chariot ahead of the rain and won.

It is easy to be critical of the "Prophet/Perceiver" motivational gift for doing things that we sometimes label as "attention getting" (John's wild appearance) when in fact they are acts of faith as directed by God. They tend to paint "pictures" through the use of illustration and their passion is an earmark of this gift.

If this gift is you or you are acquainted with a motivational gift of prophecy, you immediately recognize that this gift has a strong, intense personality with a flair for the dramatic and it is not unusual for them to proclaim the gospel utilizing odd, eccentric mannerisms.

The motivational gift of prophecy strives to be obedient to the Lord and is often passionately compelled to proclaim the message which they have received from the Lord. To them, to verbalize aloud is a matter of integrity and obedience before the Lord. To be silent is to be disobedient.

Others often misinterpret the dramatic theatrics as a need for attention or accolades from those around them. This is an understandable attitude as their mannerisms succeed in drawing attention. However the pure heart motive of the motivational prophetic gift is not to draw attention to them, but to the Word they preach. All of the drama is geared to penetrate the hearts of those around them with the message from the Lord. The heart thrust of this motivational gift is to call the sinner to repentance before God.

The Prophetic Gift Demands Fruit of Repentance:

This motivational prophetic gift delights in the fruit of repentance and the work of restoration. However, they seek "visible fruit of repentance." They demand the witness of an outward manifestation of a lifestyle change resulting from heartfelt repentance before God. They have an intense desire for outward evidences to demonstrate inward conviction. Lip service doesn't work with the motivational gift of prophecy; they look for concrete evidence of results.

The Motivational Gift of Prophecy Confronts Sin:

If you are a motivational gift of prophecy, you are uncompromising in what is right or wrong. You quickly spot and identify sin and you shun the mere thought of evil or dark shadowy behavior. You are incapable of covering over sin or rebellion and openly rebuke those that would attempt to do so. The motivational gift of prophecy confronts sin, calling a "spade a spade." Shades of gray do not exist for you. You see only "black or white." You brook no excuses, do not pet the flesh and do not allow it in others. You are a total "straight arrow."

The motivational gift of prophecy perceives everything in life from a narrow, strict viewpoint. Right and wrong are very simple matters in the mind and heart of this gift. A major flaw in this motivational gift is that their presentation may easily become harsh (because of their ability to spot and identify sin), critical (because this gift does not see any good in something that has even the smallest gray area) and condemning (because they simply do not understand why anyone would choose even the slightest compromise).

Note: It is possible to give credit to partial good and use that portion as a stepping stone to bring complete correction. This tactic encourages others to stretch to their full potential in the Lord.

A harsh, critical and condemning attitude wounds many young believers and causes harm in the Body of Christ. If you are a motivational gift of prophecy, you don't want to be a runaway freight train barreling through the congregation leaving a swath of destruction in your path. It does not matter how accurate you are if your mannerisms derail others.

Jesus is our greatest example and He confronted sin openly, yet with great love and mercy.

You must also be careful not to strip another of hope, but to encourage one another to "keep on trucking" in the Lord. God never seeks to change the believer, but to grow each one from faith to faith and glory to glory, and it is the goodness of God that brings man to repentance. Truth spoken with the love of God is the way to minister effectively to those who have compromised or fallen into sin.

Note: The answer to strengthening this weak area is to deliberately and consistently determine to allow the Holy Spirit to cultivate the fruit of agape (unconditional God kind of love) love, in everything you do.

The God kind of love is defined in 1Corinthians 13:4-8a

> "Love is patient, love is kind. It does not envy, it does not boast, it is not proud. It is not rude, it is not self-seeking, it is not easily angered, it keeps no record of wrongs. Love does not delight in evil but

27

rejoices with the truth. It always protects, always trusts, always hopes, and always perseveres. Love never fails."

No one is able to produce agape love in their own natural nature. The agape love walk is a spiritual walk. It is a work of the Holy Spirit as He grows the fruit of His love within your spirit. As you mature in the Lord, His love becomes a way of life for you.

The Prophetic Gift is Strict Concerning Personal Accountability:

This motivational gift takes responsibility for their actions and demands the same accountability in others. If you are a motivational gift of prophecy, you immediately "step up to the plate" and take ownership of your words or actions. If you are in error, you are quick to repent and take steps of restitution. This is important as before there is ever repentance, there must first be a personal acknowledgement of sin or involvement.

If this is your motivational gift, you endeavor to help others see the part they have played in their own problem. You instinctively hone in on the core of the problem and seek to bring exposure to the foundational issues. Your heart is not to place a band aid on the consequence, but to find and confront the splinter that is causing the wound to fester.

The Motivational Gift of Prophecy is Able to Empathize with Others:

If this is your motivational gift, you will find that often your heart weeps over the sin of another. That very brokenness in you will often prompt brokenness in the heart of the one that you are attempting to help. A broken and contrite heart is fertile ground for the Lord to pour out His mercy and forgiveness and to bring repentance and restoration.

Because of your empathic nature, you are able to easily identify personally with the sin or heartache of another. This can become an emotional quicksand for you as you may become laden down with the sins, afflictions or trials of others. Their pain becomes your pain. This is not God's intent. Learn to be quick to give those burdens over to the Lord. Your part is only to speak the words God gives you in the love of the Lord. You are not the Lord and He is the only One responsible to bring repentance, restoration, healing and deliverance to His children. He is the One that binds up the broken hearted and restores His Peace. He is always faithful.

The Motivational Gift of Prophecy Perseveres:

The motivational gift of prophecy is not a quitter by nature and this gift encourages others to pick themselves up in Jesus and go on in their walk with the Lord. It is important for every believer to develop the attitude of a "spiritual pit bull." Quitters never make it to the finish line, and winners simply don't know how to quit. The precious Blood of Jesus purchased the victory and this motivational prophetic gift presses on to attain it in the end.

The Prophetic Gift is Non-political:

If you are a motivational gift of prophecy, you do not possess a natural bend for diplomacy or soft pedaling. You are very direct, frank and persuasive in speaking with a tendency to strip all the "window dressing" off of a sin or situation and get down to the heart of the matter. You unceremoniously dig out the root of the problem.

You most likely don't comprehend the nuances of political maneuvers and are not adept at playing political games. You are willing to endure persecution or even ostracism when necessary in order to be obedient to the truth. The possibilities of negative reactions do not deter you. You are prepared to let "the chips fall where they may." The temptation of compromise for self-preservation is quickly rejected.

This Gift Glorifies God:

Because of the dramatic flair, this motivational gift usually draws considerable attention. However, the heart motive behind the drama is to highlight the message of God, not the messenger. As a result, a motivational gift of prophecy is uncomfortable and often embarrassed with the attention of others. They give the Glory to God. They do not seek or need a "position" or "title" to validate their identity or value before God. All that they do emanates from their personal intimacy with God.

If you are this motivational gift, you probably need to learn how to gracefully handle those moments when others give words of appreciation to you. The heart motive of others is to love you and a response is usually good manners. It is correct to simply say, "Thank you, it is the work of the Holy Spirit." This statement is true and for the motivational gift of prophecy, alleviates what often becomes for them is a "clumsy" situation.

The Motivational Gift of Prophecy bases their Life on the Word:

This motivational gift considers the Word of God the final and absolute authority. A motivational gift of prophecy utterly depends on scriptural truth to validate their authority. Their heart is to be obedient to the scriptures and their life and actions are always Word based. It is often said of them that they are a "living Bible."

The Gift of Prophecy Cares for the Reputation of God:

A motivational gift of prophecy takes great care that the Lord not be reproached for the failings of His children. If this is your motivational gift, you find that you have a deep concern for the reputation and program of the Lord. You are quick to point out that God never fails, but that people often do and that the Lord is not accountable for the free will choices that are made by His children.

This motivational gift never "blames" God for a tough situation and is not given to whining or blaming others for the challenges of life. Likewise, the motivational prophetic gift is intolerant of the whininess of others.

God is integrity; God is faithfulness; God is honorable; God is perfect all the time; God never fails. It is not right to accuse a holy God for the weaknesses of His children. When a child of God fails or goes into sin, God does not abandon that child. He will walk the troubled path with His child and offer forgiveness and restoration. He is our example on how to deal with the shortcomings of others in the Body of Christ.

The Prophetic Gift Intercedes for Others:

This motivational gift is a person of prayer and brings the needs of others before the throne of God. Their prayer thrust is mainly along the lines of repentance, restoration to God and that the Lord would bring the believer to growth and maturity. They faithfully intercede on the behalf of others in trouble.

The Gift of Prophecy is Introspective:

The motivational gift of prophecy tends to be introspective. They continually search out and examine the motives and intents of their own heart. They seek out and value correction from their peers as they have a burning desire to be right before the Lord. They tend to be very harsh on themselves and their mistakes can be devastating to them.

This motivational gift is eager to have their own blind spots pointed out to help others. They frequently use their own failings or inadequacies as examples to clarify a point. They are easily corrected as their desire is to be pure before the Lord. This gift yearns for the holiness of God.

If this is your motivational gift you have probably struggled with self- image issues. You are quick to see only your faults and failings, not your strong points or successes. You are strict with others, but hardest on yourself. "Inadequate" is most likely the word that you would use to describe how you feel. You have a tendency to strive and demand perfection in all that you do and when that fails, despair follows. The natural dramatic flair lends itself to your soul realm and even a slight misstep is often amplified in your emotions.

Balance comes by realizing that although most believers have a desire to be perfect in their endeavors; perfection is never attained on earth. That comes only as we stand in the face of perfection, which is Jesus. Your part is to give God your best effort. God's part is to supply the rest.

You will also grow in the gift that the Lord has placed within you over the process of time. Growth and maturity are natural results of time and experience.

Remember, if any work is done, it is the Lord that does the work. God sent His Son to die for humanity, and God understands the natural, the carnal, and the humanity of His children. God is always merciful and good.

The Motivational Gift of Prophecy Demands Excellence:

This motivational gift places great value in excellence and strongly urges others to cultivate the spirit of excellence in all that they do and to seek that which is totally good. Honesty in evaluating situations is inherent in their outlook, and they will be quick to see and point out that which is lacking. They maintain a strict code of ethics and demand the same in others. This gift is incapable of compromise.

The Prophetic Gift Tends to Have Problems with Personal Relationships:

The motivational gift of prophecy often experiences difficulties in their personal relationships. Their public boldness and strict standards hinder intimate personal relationships. They are hard to get to really know as they have strong walls of defense around them. They do not easily trust others. However, this gift is a loyal friend and makes friends for life.

If this is your motivational gift, your own strict code of conduct prohibits you from any unfaithfulness or treachery in your dealings with others. The godly character of others is a critical factor to you in the friendships you cultivate. Discovering a lack of character in someone you trusted as a friend automatically ends the closeness of the relationship.

If this motivational gift is you, it is a step of growth to learn not to sever the relationship when confronted with disloyalty or treachery in someone you trusted. Cordiality must remain even when closeness cannot in order to avoid conflict in the Body of Christ. Love has many expressions and you cannot help a person with their lack of ethics if you choose to abandon the relationship.

The motivational prophetic gift is also hindered by having a very private nature and it is difficult for them to learn to communicate more openly on a personal level with others. However; it is the level of communication that always dictates the level of intimacy and closeness in any relationship.

The Motivational Gift of Prophecy and Effective Communication:

Effective communication involves both speaking your heart openly and honestly and also listening to the heart of what the other is saying. The motivational gift of prophecy is sometimes weak in this area. This gift is empathetic and passionate in speaking truth and they often appear to be disinterested in hearing the viewpoint of another. This is an area that could become a problem. The solution is to work on encouraging others to share their thoughts and to develop a respectful attitude to the sometimes different or even opposing views of others. It is a sign of maturity when you can "agree to disagree" and not abandon the relationship.

Note: Often it is not the truth of the heart motive that impacts others, but it is the perception with which that truth is received. Therefore, the motivational gift of prophecy must be sensitive to the perception created by their words.

34

It is one thing to know truth; it is another to present that truth in a manner that can be easily received by others.

Motivational Gift of Prophecy in the Ditch:

A life dedicated to the Lord, and not self, becomes a balanced and fruitful life. A life dedicated to self becomes imbalanced and stuck in the ditch. When not consecrated to the Lord, this motivational gift can be a difficult personality. A motivational gift of prophecy in the ditch actually does become harsh, judgmental, critical and full of condemnation. The weakness takes over. Because this motivational gift is such a strong personality, they can greatly wound others when not surrendered to the Lord. To compensate for this weakness, it is important to refuse to receive offense, and to live a lifestyle of submission to God and forgiveness towards others.

Also, this motivational gift in the natural can attempt to "correct" the life of another. This can go into manipulation or control, and even if the motive is for the good of another, it is not a godly or scriptural course of action. All forms of control or manipulation are rooted in witchcraft and are a stench in the nostrils of God.

These are areas that require monitoring. All true correction comes through the work of the Holy Spirit. Only God grows His children. This motivational gift must always acknowledge the limitations on the responsibility given by the Lord. They are only responsible for the message God gives. God is responsible for results and God never over-rides the free will choices of another.

Professional Strengths of This Motivational Gift:

- If you are a motivational gift of prophecy, you are adept at public speaking and you express yourself well verbally.

- You are able to formulate and execute a well-defined business plan.

- You are able to identify and document goals and the stepping stones needed to reach those goals.

- You are quick to discern the motives of business associates and you have a knack for hiring the right person for the right job.

- You adhere to a strict ethical standard and shun the appearance of compromise.

- You strictly adhere to rules, regulations and authority structures and you have no problem submitting to rightful authority.

- This motivational gift does not shirk from confrontation when necessary, and addresses issues frankly and bluntly.

- You are probably very direct in verbal or written communication.

- The motivational gift of prophecy is usually open to suggestions for the betterment of the plan and to focus on the goals and this gift will usually take the opinions of others into serious consideration.

Some of the Secular Professional Aptitudes of the Motivational Gift of Prophecy:

Air Traffic Controller	Ambassador
Inspector	Judge
Lawyer	Scientist
Reporter	Philosopher
Paramedic	Criminologist
Life Insurance Agent	Guidance Counselor
Market Researcher/Analyst	Military Officer

Motivational Gift of Server

Chapter 3

The Motivational Gift of Server/Helper is a person of action. They demonstrate their love in deeds (acts of service) rather than words. The server enjoys living a life of service to others.

Those who are called to be server/helpers are a blessing and are invaluable to the church body. Without them, no church could function well. The need to serve is so inherent in this gift that they are not fulfilled until they have a place to serve.

The Motivational Gift of Serving is a Practical Personality:

The revealing earmark of the motivational gift of serving is that they are practical and down to earth in everything they do and they especially enjoy manual projects, jobs and functions.

If you are this motivational gift, you are very alert and quick, and intuitively hone in on even the practical needs that go unnoticed by most. However; you are often oblivious of the emotional or spiritual needs around you.

You most likely rate serving as the first and foremost thing in your life. This motivational gift tends to view meeting the practical needs as foundational to meeting the emotional or spiritual needs of others. The reasoning is "to prepare for the ministry to the emotional or spiritual realm by first attending to the practical needs of the natural realm." Before you would witness to a homeless person, you would probably want to give him something to eat. Through your serving, you demonstrate in a practical way the reality of God's love. "Fill the belly so you can then feed the soul" aptly paints a clear picture of the heart motive of the serving gift.

One common misunderstanding concerning the motivational serving gift is that they are often considered "unspiritual" because they are so focused on the practical side of life.

Prayer is the answer to this misconception. When a motivational gift of serving is following the leading of the Holy Spirit, they must be careful not be offended if their motives are misconstrued. The fruit of longsuffering brings peace. Each of us is often misunderstood. It is a point of maturity to remain in love even though our actions (or spirituality) may be misinterpreted.

Note: One of the reasons for this study in the motivational gifts is to shed the light of truth on the various gifts created by God. The motivational serving gift is handcrafted by our Lord to serve in the arena of practical needs. This is the purpose of this motivational gift. The server excels in fulfilling their role in the Body of Christ by detecting and meeting practical needs. This is the active manifestation of the spiritual motivational gift placed within them by the Lord.

Martha is an excellent example of the motivational gift of serving. Even with the Master in the house, she was focused on meeting His practical needs. It did not occur to her to receive anything from Him, and she became frustrated with Mary for not helping her with the serving.

> "Now it came to pass, as they went, that he entered into a certain village: and a certain woman named Martha received him into her house. And she had a sister called Mary, which also sat at Jesus' feet, and heard his word. But Martha was cumbered about much serving, and came to him, and said, Lord, dost thou not care that my sister hath left me to serve alone? Bid her therefore that she help me. And Jesus answered and said unto her, Martha, Martha, thou art careful and troubled about many things: But one thing is needful: and Mary hath chosen that good part, which shall not be taken away from her." Luke 10:38-42

John 11 describes Martha accompanying Jesus to the tomb where her brother, Lazarus, was laid. Everything Martha saw and commented on revealed her as a motivational gift of serving. Even as Jesus was preparing to call Lazarus forth, Martha saw only the practical side of the situation. Her comment was that after four days, her brother "stank." She was so concerned about the smell, she completely missed the fact that a miracle was about to take place. Motivational Gifts of Serving are down to earth and practical and those qualities were exemplified in Martha.

The Serving Gift Takes Initiative:

If you are a motivational gift of serving, you will instantly see what needs to be done without being told and you are happy to do it. You probably would be uneasy with leaving a practical need unmet.

The Motivational Gift of Serving is Naturally Hospitable:

This gift is naturally hospitable (remember Martha) and tends to view hospitality as an opportunity to show their love through serving. They are able to portray warmth and acceptance to those that they serve.

Servers are Detail Oriented:

If you are the motivational gift of serving, you are blessed with an eye for details that make others feel welcomed and appreciated. You have the unusual ability to note and recall specific likes and dislikes that others would not even notice, and you effortlessly put details and individuals together. For instance, you will automatically remember how a person prefers their coffee and you will serve coffee to them perfectly prepared to their taste. That person will never forget how your love and acceptance was demonstrated to them in a very practical way.

The Motivational Gift of Serving is a Hard Worker:

This motivational gift sees a need and goes to work on that need as quickly as possible. The motivational serving gift does not like to leave a task unfinished and will work without regard to personal weariness. They push to get it done.

Since motivational gifts of serving usually want to finish a task before they go home, many times they put in long arduous hours to order to complete the work. This intense "drive to finish" can in itself give rise to several areas of concern.

First, the "workaholic" tendency in the motivational gift of serving often takes precedent over their family responsibilities. If you are a motivational serving gift, you will have to strive to attain and maintain a godly order concerning your work and the care of your family. God is the only One Who sets the order of priorities for His children, and that order is God first, family second and work or ministry, third. In the eyes of God, your family and home must come ahead of your work. This can be particularly difficult for the serving gift as a major part of meeting the needs of the family is to spend quality time with them and be there for them. It is a growth process to learn to discipline yourself to put the well-being of your family ahead of your compulsion to complete a task. This is an area that the motivational gift of serving must continually monitor. It easily creeps into imbalance and can bring devastating results.

Secondly, you need to be sensitive in this area concerning your co-workers or your team. They must meet the needs of their families also. The motivational serving gift must learn to not be critical of others when they feel they must leave and gracefully excuse them with the love of the Lord.

Thirdly, motivational gifts of serving normally possess a high energy level and they are driven to finish their task. As a result, the drive and stamina of a motivational server may be intimidating to others on their team. The motivational serving gift has a tendency to be demanding and "push to get it done" without regard to their personal weariness or the physical endurance of their individual team members. Problems arise if they become critical when a co-worker is not able to keep up with them.

Note: The motivational serving gift is wonderful and gracious to a person they are serving, however; they are not noted for tact or diplomacy with their co-workers. Their focus is honed in on their current project, not the people laboring with them in that project. Motivational servers may unconsciously view their co-workers as "objects to use" to get the job done and overlook the individual personalities involved. This is a cause of dissension, often creating resentment in those around them.

Since the natural flow of the motivational serving gift is toward the task and not the people involved with them in the task, once they begin a project they tend to develop "tunnel vision." They "see" only the work and can become oblivious to the people that are involved with them in the work. It follows naturally that their co-workers may begin to feel "used and abused" and become disgruntled with the server. This is fertile ground for conflict to grow and the entire project could be placed in danger of becoming entangled in a quagmire of negative emotions.

In order to avoid a multitude of possible repercussions, the motivational gift of serving must recognize and label this weakness as a potential problem area. The answer is to deliberately seek to develop a greater sensitivity in their relationship and mannerisms with their co-workers. Extra care should be given to verbally acknowledge and appreciate the help that others bring to the table.

The Motivational Gift of Serving Sees the Short Range Vision:

A motivational gift of serving tends to enjoys short range goals more than long range goals. They see immediate needs (which are usually short range) rather than the whole picture (which usually includes the long range objective). They focus on the present need, not the complete objective.

If this is your motivational gift, you receive a sense of great satisfaction and tremendous enjoyment in meeting short-range goals. However, you will most likely feel frustrated and even overwhelmed when presented with a long-range goal. There is a solution to this problem. For a motivational gift of serving to tackle a long range project without frustration, they must learn to first divide it into several slices of short range goals. One slice at a time becomes "do-able."

Also, since long range goals are not the arena that is inherent in the motivational gift of serving, it is important to recognize and acknowledge where the gifting begins and ends. There is nothing lacking in a motivational serving gift that does not flow with long range visions. They are gifted to accomplish the necessary daily needs and over the process of time, they are invaluable to the long range vision.

Servers Are Uncomfortable with Time Limits on Tasks:

This motivational gift can become intensely pressured with time limits on jobs. The motivational serving gift is intent in every minute detail of a task, and their desire is to complete a work to perfection. Sometimes that can require more time than is available. This is especially difficult for the server gift as they are compelled to consistently go "above and beyond" in everything they do.

If this is your motivational gift, you are diligent and faithful to accomplish whatever task is assigned to you. You want to see a job done well and you will do extra work to accomplish it. When completed, your work exhibits a spirit of excellence.

The Motivational Gift of Serving is Organized:

Most motivational gifts of serving are organized and orderly in their work areas. This attribute is invaluable to accomplishing the task at hand and enables the actual work to go smoothly; however, their penchant for organization often reveals a sticking point in the personality of the motivational server.

This motivational gift keeps everything in meticulous order and they can become very upset if anyone disturbs that order. They can be hard to work with as they don't really want another person in their personal domain. They have a tendency to "commandeer" their area of service. For example, you may find that a motivational gift of serving that is over kitchen detail may view the kitchen as "theirs," and resent others going through drawers to look for something. Because of this, these motivational gifts often have a hard time with close working relationships with others.

If you are a motivational gift of serving, you probably need to give special attention as to how your words or mannerisms are perceived by those that work with you. Often, it is not the actual intent or heart motive that causes strife or hurt feelings in others, but it is how you are received. You may find that you need to soften your approach.

There are areas in each of the motivational gifts that require tempering. A group of motivational gifts of serving together can easily become "Too many Chiefs and not enough Indians." Through your relationship with the Lord, you can mature into the fullness of the gift that He created you to be. It is the work of the Holy Spirit to grow the fruit of the Spirit within each child of God. Loving manners and kind words will bring peace and joy to any team united in a common goal. Usually learning to work with others successfully does not come automatically with this gift, but requires walking it out over a process of time. Everyone has a natural side and flesh has a loud voice. The most productive and fulfilling relationships are always the result of hard work and dying to self.

Servers Find it Difficult to Say "No":

The motivational serving gift has a tendency to feel "personally responsible" for all that needs to be done. If you are this motivational gift, you will probably agree to a request without thinking rather than risk disappointing another. As a result it is common for the motivational serving gift to commit to more tasks than is humanly possible to accomplish.

Their reluctance to decline a task is the reason that this gift is usually involved in a lot of projects. This can be a problem area, as this motivational gift can become overwhelmed with the sheer mountain of commitments that they tend to make.

Several problems arise because of this overwhelming feeling of being personally responsible to fulfill every need. First, there are only so many commitments that any one person can fulfill. That leaves some tasks undone, which in turn creates tremendous guilt in the mind of the motivational serving gift. Also, the tasks that were not completed may place undue pressure on others. Even though you may be ordained a motivational gift of serving by the Lord that does not mean that every task is your personal assignment from God. Learn to seek His face about exactly what is your personal project and what He has intended for another.

If you are a motivational gift of serving, learn to place boundaries on your time. Your time must be balanced between your family and your commitments. There must also be some unscheduled time left for you so that you don't completely "burn out."

It is okay to say "No," when you are asked to commit to a task that you feel is not for you. Refuse to be manipulated by the wants and needs of others and carefully choose your commitments. You will find that you will ultimately be angry with yourself and others and feelings of resentment will fester within you if you allow yourself to be coerced into a task that you do not feel is yours to do.

Many times, motivational servers that do not learn to say "no' will become discouraged by all the "busyness" and will even leave the church in order to "take back their life."

Note: If you are a motivational serving gift that is in a leadership position, know the ones that you ask to do a task. Make it your business to know what they have already obligated themselves to do. Never allow the motivational serving gifts under you to commit to an overload. Learning to choose which requests to take and which to refuse comes with time and experience. Some will not be there yet.

This Gift May Clash with Bureaucracy:

The motivational gift of serving can clash with the "bureaucracy." They are often impatient about "going through channels" and will many times use personal funds or do jobs themselves to avoid delay in meeting a need or completing a task. This can create a myriad of problems.

First, in order for any home, church, project, place of employment, etc. to function well, there are directives in place. There is always a "chain of command." As the motivational serving gift matures, they also learn the importance of operating within the rules. It is a foundational ingredient of teamwork. Those at the top of the chain are on the same team, and clearly defined rules are a blessing to all concerned.

Secondly, bypassing others fosters the feeling that they are not needed or welcome. Truthfully, every member of the team is important and each has a contribution that is beneficial to the finished project.

Thirdly, in the financial realm, bypassing proper channels can wreak havoc with the budget. A motivational server will often take it upon themselves to pay for things that come up unexpectedly out of their own pockets. Their reasoning is that this will expedite the completion of the project and they expect to be reimbursed. Sometimes those unexpected expenses are not calculated in the anticipated cost.

A fourth problem with this is that when leadership is not consulted, confusion can arise. It may become a scene where the "left hand does not know what the right hand is doing."

Note: There are those who mistakenly believe that rebellion is the root of this problem. This is an untrue and unfair assessment of the heart motive of this motivational gift. The motivational serving gift is naturally innovative, resourceful, and self-reliant and they are not afraid of hard work. Problem solving is so inherent in this gift, if presented with an unexpected need or problem in completing a task, it never occurs to them to stop what they are doing in order to obtain permission or approval from others. They naturally set about fixing the problem or meeting the need. They tend to be "Lone Rangers" until they mature in their gifting.

If this is your motivational gift, this is can be a double edged sword. On the one hand, you are extremely well equipped to handle an unexpected glitch in your assigned task without consulting others; on the other hand, teamwork requires communication. Also, those that are over you depend on you to either consult with them or follow the plan. Any deviation may impact the entire project. As you grow in your motivational gifting you will learn to think "team work." It is a learned discipline to include others and build a team.

The Motivational Gift of Serving is Often Misconstrued:

It is not uncommon for a motivational serving gift to be misunderstood by others. Their obvious eagerness to serve is often misconstrued as attempting to self-promote or to advance their own agenda.

This is not true in the heart motive of the motivational server, however; it is a perception that others may have of them. Jealousies, wounded feelings, even conflict can arise in those around them. This is easily avoided by letting others know that they are included in the task. Developing a strong, united team also goes a long way in alleviating this misconception.

The Motivational Gift of Serving Finds it Hard to Stay on Course:

The motivational serving gift can be caught up in "moment by moment" situations. As a result, it is very easy for a server to become side-tracked with the needs of others and detour from the boss's (or pastor's) directions. This easily causes a "domino effect" of ramifications impacting all concerned.

If this is your motivational gift, you will grow in your gifting and in adhering to the task at hand. This is not always easy as you are constantly aware of any practical need that crops up around you and you probably feel compelled to "put out the fires." You will learn to recognize and resist distractions.

The Serving Gift Easily Enables Others:

If you are a motivational serving gift, there are times that you may be tempted to rush to meet a need that has come to your attention. Your desire to help may interfere with what the Lord is doing in the life of another. Each of us faces seasons of difficulties at times, however; God grows and matures His children through the tribulations of life and He walks the fiery trials with them.

Avoid this mistake by taking the time to pray and seek God's face before you rush to the rescue. The Holy Spirit will be quick to lead you in the role He would have you play in dealing with the needs of others in the Body of Christ. You may unintentionally become an enabler if you do not allow the Lord to have His perfect way.

The Motivational Gift of Serving Must Cultivate Understanding of Other Gifts:

Normally, the motivational gift of serving has little understanding or tolerance for anyone that does not share the same ability to spot and meet practical needs. However; we are not all the same motivational gift. Every child of God is unique and has been given an individual purpose and destiny, and the Lord has equipped each one of us with the precise motivational gift needed to fulfill the plan of

God for our life. As we grow and mature in the Lord, we learn to accept and embrace the different gifts in others.

Serving Gifts Intensely Need the Appreciation of Others:

The motivational gift of serving has an intense inner need to be truly appreciated for their contribution. Motivational servers are honest and straightforward by nature and instantly spot any form of pretense or insincerity while being thanked for their work.

Emotionally, their service is often connected with the value they place on themselves. They have a tendency to try to work hard in order to validate their importance and to earn the love of others.

The motivational server's need for appreciation often results in wounded feelings. A motivational serving gift can easily feel that they are taken advantage of when they are not continually thanked and verbally appreciated for their work. This can become a point of offense and fertile ground that breeds contention.

The solution is for the motivational gift to continually present their service as an offering to their Heavenly Father and know that the Lord is blessed by their faithfulness in serving.

God judges the motive and intent of the heart. All that we do should be as unto the Lord, not unto man. God sees all that is sown into the work of His Kingdom and He rewards openly.

Is Uncomfortable Being Served by Others:

As a general rule, the motivational gift of server finds it very difficult to receive service from others. They can cheerfully wash the feet of others, but often experience feelings of embarrassment by having their own feet washed by another.

Jesus is our example and He received as well as gave. The woman with the alabaster box anointed His feet with the precious ointment and Jesus corrected His disciples for rebuking her.

We are all part of one Body of Christ, and giving and receiving are principles of God. It is a step in spiritual growth for a motivational serving gift to learn to gracefully receive service from another. Also, others are blessed as they are given opportunity to serve. If that service is refused, that person may be robbed of the blessing that comes from that gift of service.

Motivational Gift of Serving in the Ditch:

A motivational gift of serving off in a ditch can become bossy, demanding, controlling and even sharp tongued. In this condition, they can wreak havoc in a work rather than a blessing. To compensate, they must take extra care that they are sensitive to the feelings of those around them and present themselves in a loving manner.

The serving gift that is imbalanced is easily offended. If their need for appreciation and verbal "kudos" is not met to their satisfaction it can create intense resentment and discontentment within them. They can grumble loudly and stir up conflict in the Body of Christ. The way to compensate for this weakness is for the server to continually remind themselves that all work done is unto the Lord, and that it is the Lord that sees and rewards openly. As with all gifts, daily intimacy with the Lord keeps this gift balanced and fruitful.

Professional Aptitudes of This Motivational Gift:

- In the business world and in the church, secretaries often tend to be motivational serving gifts. In the church, you will also find that many ushers have the motivational gift of serving.

- Motivational serving gifts can sense the things that need to be done, and they will do them without being asked or prodded. They will often do more than asked. They will seek out the practical need and fill it. For example, this gift would easily remember to co-ordinate the boss's itinerary and make and confirm all necessary reservations.

- A motivational gift of serving usually keeps everything in meticulous order. They would see that all tools were clean and organized, the supplies were neatly stocked and that all equipment was routinely maintained

- This motivational gift delights in serving and doesn't usually complain about running errands, coming to work early, staying late and using personal time to complete a task For a motivational serving gift, usually no job is too small or too big to ask of them.

Some of the Secular Professional Aptitudes of the Motivational Gift of Serving are:

Accountant   Librarian

Architect	Nurse
Auditor	Geographer
Mathematician	Bank Teller
Builder	Postman
Bus Driver	Plumber
Metal Worker	Carpenter
Secretary	Receptionist
Civil Servant	Cashier/Checker
Assembly Worker	Computer Programmer
Mechanical Drawing	

Motivational Gift of Teacher

Chapter 4

The Motivational Gift of Teacher is not to be confused with the Office Gift of Teacher. They are two separate categories of gifting and the Motivational Teaching Gift may or may not stand in the Office Gift of Teacher.

The motivational gift of teacher is vital to the church body. All of their lessons are equally well prepared and solidly founded in biblical truths. They are able to bring the same excellence to the children's ministry as well as to the adults.

This gift enjoys deep, systematic study and training. In their search for in depth meaning, the teaching gift could be likened to a gold miner. The miner can use a pan in a stream and find grains of gold, but he knows if he wants to hit the "Mother Lode" he has to work hard and dig deeper. The gift of teacher delights in doing just that.

Paul is one of the greatest examples of a motivational gift of teaching in the Bible. His mannerisms and character traits reveal he was a motivational gift of teaching even before he had a personal revelation of the Lord.

Before he encountered Jesus, he lived as a Pharisee, a well-educated man of power and authority and he was well known for his knowledge and penchant for in-depth studies. He had an established reputation for his knowledge of the Law and Jewish customs. The scriptures reveal that he was also well versed in Roman law. He often stated his rights as a Roman citizen.

"And as they bound him with thongs, Paul said unto the centurion that stood by, 'Is it lawful for you to scourge a man that is a Roman, and uncondemned?' When the centurion heard that, he went and told the chief captain, saying, 'Take heed what thou doest: for this man is a Roman.'" Acts 22:25-26

"And the keeper of the prison told this saying to Paul, The magistrates have sent to let you go: now therefore depart, and go in peace. But Paul said unto them, They have beaten us openly uncondemned, being Romans, and have cast us into prison; and now do they thrust us out privately? nay verily; but let them come themselves and fetch us out. And the sergeants told these words unto the magistrates: and they feared, when they heard that they were Romans." Acts 16:36-38

Paul also studied the customs and beliefs of the various Gentile cultures. When he was in Corinth, he addressed the issues that were common to the area. When he was addressing Greeks, he knew their mannerisms and ministered to them in a way they could receive. He was not afraid of controversy and he was adept at skillfully debating with all manner of peoples.

"For all the Athenians and strangers which were there spent their time in nothing else, but either to tell, or to hear some new thing.) Then Paul stood in the midst of Mars' hill, and said, Ye men of Athens, I perceive that in all things ye are too superstitious. For as I passed by, and beheld your devotions, I found an altar with this inscription, TO THE

UNKNOWN GOD. Whom therefore ye ignorantly worship, him declare I unto you." Acts 17:21-23

After Paul's encounter with Jesus, Galatians states that he was fourteen years in preparation for the ministry assignment he had received from God.

"But when it pleased God, who separated me from my mother's womb, and called me by his grace, To reveal his Son in me, that I might preach him among the heathen; immediately I conferred not with flesh and blood: Neither went I up to Jerusalem to them which were apostles before me; but I went into Arabia, and returned again unto Damascus. Then after three years I went up to Jerusalem to see Peter, and abode with him fifteen days. But other of the apostles saw I none, save James the Lord's brother. Now the things which I write unto you, behold, before God, I lie not. Afterwards I came into the regions of Syria and Cilicia; And was unknown by face unto the churches of Judaea which were in Christ: But they had heard only, That he which persecuted us in times past now preaches the faith which once he destroyed. And they glorified God in me." Galatians 1:15-21

Then fourteen years after I went up again to Jerusalem with Barnabas, and took Titus with me also." Galatians 2:1

Everything about Paul's personality reveals all of the earmarks of the Motivational Gift of Teaching. He could be presented as the poster child of this particular gifting.

The Teaching Gift Is Intellectual:

The motivational teaching gift is extremely intelligent and they easily comprehend complicated in-depth study material. It is almost as though they assimilate knowledge through osmosis. As a result of their sharp mental acuity, they can have a tendency to depend on their intellect and their research rather than the leading of the Holy Spirit. However; "rhema (revealed) knowledge" of the Word does not come through natural intellect or even extensive research. Revelation knowledge comes forth only by the work of the Holy Spirit, not the efforts of man.

This Gift is a Prolific Reader:

This motivational gift is a prolific reader and enjoys deep "word studies." They possess an insatiable hunger for truth. They place great emphasis on the complete accuracy of words and normally cross-reference with various sources to glean every possible particle of truth.

The Motivational Gift of Teaching is an Avid Researcher:

Every person is different, but there are inherent traits within each gift that identify the gifting. The earmark of the motivational gift of teaching is that they are by nature true researchers. They are compelled to dig deeply for truth.

If you are this motivational gift, you find that you easily "get lost" in your research and you love to spend hours on end with your "nose in the books." When you research a word or scripture, you are not satisfied until you have exhausted every possible reference available. You most likely run references on every word in a scripture verse in order to obtain complete accuracy. You have a tendency to meticulously dig out every grain of truth, and then you will run references to assure that the integrity of the original context is maintained.

You probably place little or no credence in any source that is not Bible or an established, reputable Bible study help. You are not comfortable with and tend to avoid any illustrations taken from a non-biblical source.

You are also greatly resistant to a scriptural illustration taken out of context. You tend to be a stickler for details and you have a great respect for God's Word. You instinctively strive to maintain the integrity of the Bible.

The Teaching Gift Always Validates New Truths:

The motivational teacher gift is Word based and they are overjoyed when they are able to discover, prove and confirm a Bible truth. This motivational gift also delights in researching to validate a truth they already know.

The motivational teaching gift finds it necessary to validate any new information or revelation they find using already established systems of truth. Before this motivational gift is comfortable with new information, they meticulously verify it through several sources using caution so as to maintain contextual integrity.

They are thrilled when they uncover a deeper revelation of the truth through their Word studies.

The Motivational Gift of Teacher is Systematic in Presentation:

The motivational gift of teaching usually presents the truth they have discovered in a very systematic sequence. They tend to build one fact upon another. It could be likened to a lawyer building a case. They are adept in painting a clear picture of the topic they are teaching by utilizing the biblical principle of line upon line and precept upon precept.

The Teaching Gift Believes Their Gift is Primary:

The motivational gift of teacher believes that their gift is the foundation for all other gifts. They place such a high value on the truth that they discover through their research, they often to feel that their gift is the most important and primary gift. They are "Word orientated" and their priority is accuracy and knowledge in the Word of God.

Note: This motivational gift often struggles with issues of pride because of their deep studies and immense amount of sheer knowledge.

For the Motivational Gift of Teaching Research is First Love, Teaching is Second:

If this is your motivational gift, you will find that you receive greater joy in the researching of a lesson than in the actual presentation of the lesson. You most likely relate more to the study itself than to the people you teach. The teaching of the lesson probably feels anti-climactic to you.

This has its' drawbacks as you usually become so focused on and place such emphasis on the accuracy of scriptural interpretation that your teaching may lack warmth and relevancy. You may neglect to give adequate instructions as to how your students may successfully apply those principles to their everyday life situations.

For any child of God to grow in the Lord, they must not only know the truth of God, but understand the practical application of that truth. To quote the Word is not enough. One must be able to apply the principles in the Word to the actual challenges of life.

"And you shall know the truth, and the truth shall make you free." John 8:33

According to this scripture, it is not the truth alone that will set the captive free. It is the truth that is **known** (revealed and understood) to the individual child of God that brings the liberty of the Lord. Therefore it is not enough for you as a motivational teaching gift to research and accumulate a vast knowledge of truth, but you also must endeavor to present that knowledge in a manner that may be effectively utilized by your students.

Note: Teaching is the impartation of knowledge. It is about your ability to break down what you know into bite sized pieces for your students. If your students are not assimilating the truth that you speak of, it would be prudent to pray and seek the help of the Holy Spirit with your manner of presentation. It is the Holy Spirit and the Word together that bring the life of God to the student. The wise motivational teaching gift relies heavily on the Holy Spirit when presenting their lesson.

This Gift is Easily Sidetracked:

This motivational gift can be easily sidetracked by new interests. Many times it is a stretch to stay on course. However; it is a lesson that all need to learn, even the motivational teacher gift. It is a point of growth, faithfulness and integrity.

Critiques Other Teachers:

This motivational gift has a penchant for testing the knowledge of other teachers. They are constantly comparing their level of knowledge to the level of knowledge of other teachers. They possess an inherent tendency to "grade" or critique other teachers rather than listen to the heart of the message.

Note: Any attempt to test another believer's knowledge does not come from a right heart motive. It is prideful and devalues and demeans other believers or teachers. Also, the need to constantly compete is rooted in the natural or carnal nature and is antagonistic to a life in and of the Spirit. An earmark of a heart that is surrendered to God is unity and we become unified through the fruit of unconditional love.

The Motivational Gift of Teacher Has Difficulty Receiving Teaching from Others:

The motivational teaching gift finds it easy to dismiss other teaching gifts. As a result, it may be difficult for the motivational gift of teaching to enjoy or to receive from the teaching of another.

Motivational teaching gifts must take care that they remain teachable. Any teacher that teaches by the leading of the Holy Spirit will bring forth something for every person in attendance. A person that is preaching or teaching their very first sermon or lesson is able to minister to most seasoned teachers if their heart is open to receive from God. A heart that cannot be taught is a heart full of pride, and God always resists the proud.

Areas of Concern:

There are two weak areas that are common in the motivational gift of teacher. Because of the vast knowledge they have acquired through research and study, the motivational teaching gift has a tendency to have issues with pride. This becomes evident in their "grading" other teachers and comparing the knowledge of others with their own. Rather than embrace another teacher as a peer and share the truths they have discovered, they often critique others. This is a heart attitude that can cause one to become un-teachable and therefore unreachable.

Pride also may be the factor in this motivational gift's difficulty receiving correction from any authority over them. Competition, conflict and envy are by-products of pride. The solution is for the motivational teaching gift to continually focus on the Lord as their source of success and victory. More of God and less of self is their answer.

The second weakness is that the motivational gift of teaching is so strongly focused on the Word of God that they forget to factor in the work of the Holy Spirit. Those who are only Word oriented have a tendency to become legalistic, even sometimes harsh or critical. Those who are only Holy Spirit oriented have a tendency to become imbalanced and "flaky." It takes both the Word of God and the leading of the Holy Spirit to walk in the fullness of God and to be the blessing that the Lord intended.

Motivational Gift of Teaching in a Ditch:

A motivational gift of teaching in a ditch may become harsh, critical, arrogant and abrasive. Also, in this condition, they do not receive correction easily.

As with all of the gifts when surrendered to the Lord, the many wonderful attributes that are inherent within the motivational gift of teaching greatly enrich the Body of Christ.

Professional Aptitudes of This Motivational Gift:

- The motivational teaching gift is well equipped and motivated to write a program, explain it and train people in it, but they are not usually interested in running the business or selling the product.

- While they especially enjoy the researching for the creation of the program, they prefer to teach someone else how to do the "hands on application" so that they can move on to the next research challenge.

- They excel in the areas of systematic training, seminar teaching, consulting, and research.

- This motivational gift enjoys developing programs, but loses interest when it comes time to institute it. Their joy is derived from the research and development of the program. They are especially delighted when one that they have taught has great success with a program they developed. Again, their delight is in the program as it is their "baby." They cheerfully leave the successful institution of that program to others.

- There are times that their systematic approach is not practical. It is important for the motivational teaching gift to be able to adapt to the parameters of the task at hand.

The Motivational Gift of Teaching especially excels as:

Anthropologist   Journalist   Psychiatrist
Archaeologist   Librarian   Psychologist;
Astronomer   Biologist   Chemist
Scientist   Geologist   Curator
Meteorologist;   Medical Technologist
Reporter   Engineer   Physicist
Proof-reader   Nutritionist   Surgeon
Chiropractor   Oceanographer
College Professor   Computer Programmer

Theologian   Composer   Optometrist;
Researcher/Analyst   Physician   Writer
Pharmacist   Botanist   Philosopher
Language Teacher   History/Math Teacher
Bible Teacher   Research Scientist
Researcher   School Administrator

Motivational Gift of Exhortation

Chapter 5

The Motivational Gift of Exhortation is a joy to all that are blessed by their presence. This motivational gift always sees the best in everyone and seeks to find the pearl in every situation. Exhorters have a positive attitude and are continually encouraging everyone around them.

If this is your motivational gift, you wholeheartedly believe in victorious living and have a deep desire to see that the Word "becomes flesh" in the lives of others. You are continually edifying, comforting, strengthening and urging others to "keep on trucking." You encourage the weary to "go another step."

The Motivational Gift of Exhortation Loves People:

An earmark of this motivational gift is that they love people. If this is your motivational gift, you are a "people person," and you depend on being accepted when speaking to others. You may even become frustrated if you meet with resistance as your motivation is to help them. You are also a "problem solver," and once a problem becomes known to you, you immediately get to work formulating a practical, workable solution.

Silas and Barnabas were both motivational gifts of exhortation and they give us glimpses into the personality traits that are inherent within this motivational gift. Silas encouraged others in the Lord, and he praised and worshipped the Lord continually. He was a continual blessing to Paul.

> "And Judas and Silas, being prophets also themselves, exhorted the brethren with many words, and confirmed them." Acts 15:32

> "And at midnight Paul and Silas prayed, and sang praises unto God: and the prisoners heard them." Acts 16:25

The motivational gift of exhortation was so defined in Barnabas that he was actually called "the son of encouragement" in Acts 4:36. He continually, instinctively exhorted all around him.

> "Then tidings of these things came unto the ears of the church which was in Jerusalem: and they sent forth Barnabas that he should go as far as Antioch. Who, when he came, and had seen the grace of God, was glad, and exhorted them all, that with purpose of heart they would cleave unto the Lord." Acts 11:22-23 *KJV*

The Exhorter Finds the Blessing in Every Trial:

If you are the motivational gift of exhortation, you have the uncanny knack of perceiving how tribulation can be a benefit and produce new levels of maturity. You perceive blessings in the challenges of life.

The Motivational Gift of Exhortation Only Sees Victory:

If you are a motivational gift of exhortation, you see victorious conquest when a new battle arises and are able to believe God for the miraculous even in impossible situations. You are not a complainer, and have a difficult time with the whining of others. Defeat is never an option to you, as you see God as well able to bring victory no matter what the situation.

This Gift is Practical:

The motivational gift of exhortation is on the practical side. They have a tendency to avoid or reject systems of information that lack a practical application.

The motivational gift of exhortation possesses keen insight into Bible principles and they are gifted with the ability to translate the truth of God's Word into a step by step road map to victorious living. Their solution is both easy to understand and to implement. It is a "how the rubber meets the road" application to everyday life situations.

Needs Practical Application:

The exhorter actually experiences a sense of grief when teaching doesn't have a practical application. Even while hearing a teaching, this gift is already visualizing a practical application and they become disappointed in a teacher that does not reveal how to utilize biblical principles in life situations. A gift of exhortation will probably not sit under that teacher again.

This Gift Delights in Helping Others:

The motivational exhorter gift is overjoyed when they are able to see a person take their counsel and begin to utilize their recommended "steps of action" to meet a need or solve a problem. They also may become agitated or unhappy if their solutions are not received.

If this motivational gift is you, you must learn to release the problems of others to the Lord and not take it personally when another rejects your advice or plan. It is between that person and God.

The Motivational Gift of Exhortation Needs Results:

If this is your motivational gift, you find great delight in meetings or personal conferences that produce results. You need to see the fruit of your work.

Not Competitive by Nature:

This motivational gift is not competitive by nature and is open to receiving new insights from a different prospective. When two motivational exhorter gifts meet, they happily exchange plans and ideas and glean the best from each other. They are naturally accepting of another exhorter.

Is Non-judgmental:

The motivational exhorter gift is able to accept people as they are without feeling the need to judge them. They don't seem to see prejudicial differences in people, and most are comfortable in their presence. They absolutely don't make any distinction between rich or poor, clean or dirty, nor culture or class. They just love people and are as happy praying with the drunk on the street as the saint in the church house.

The Motivational Gift of Exhortation Interacts Well with Others:

This motivational gift is a happy gift and interacts easily with others. Times spent bouncing ideas and thoughts off others bring special enjoyment.

Emphasizes Steps of Action:

If this is your motivational gift, you probably place great emphasis on simple steps of action; however this manner of presenting your solution may seem to a person in distress as over-simplifying their problem.

A person that is in the midst of crisis needs to know that you comprehend the complexity of their situation before he is able to receive the "steps of action" that you give. If you are to help, you must hear not only the words they speak, but the beat of their heart. "Listening" is not inherent in the motivational exhorter gift, but rather a learned discipline.

The motivational gift of exhortation is short on empathy and sees the practical side of the problem and not always the "human side." They encourage without empathizing. In order for this motivational gift to come to full potential, there can be a need to allow the Holy Spirit to develop their sensitivity to the feelings and emotions of others. Ministry encompasses the whole man, not just the problems of man.

The Motivational Gift of Exhortation Envisions Solutions:

This motivational gift is able to clearly "envision" how their recommended steps can lead to a successful solution to a problem. This gift can be coercive and become urgent; even forceful when giving steps of action. This stems from the intensity of their desire to help. This is an area that requires monitoring as this tendency is only a step away from appearing controlling or manipulative.

The Lord is never in a hurry. A more correct way to present the solution is through praying with the one in the situation and openly seeking the wisdom and timing of the Lord. The exhorter gift must take care to bring the Lord into the steps of action.

The Exhorter Gift Worships God:

Exhorter gifts are worshippers by nature and live a life of praise to God. They continually acknowledge and worship the Lord.

The heart motive of the motivational exhorter gift is normally very humble before the throne of God. That humility is evidenced as this gift gives praise and Glory to God.

This Gift is a Living Witness to God:

If this motivational gift is you, you tend to believe the most effective way to win non-Christians to the Lord is by being a living example. Your very lifestyle is a reflection of your deep faith in God; however others may perceive this viewpoint as an excuse to avoid witnessing to the lost through personal evangelism.

While it is true that you are the only Bible that many will read, it is also true that the Holy Spirit sets before us divine appointments. Developing in sensitivity to the leading of the Holy Spirit may many times open a door of opportunity for you to witness of the goodness of God to another. God uses His people in many ways to win others to Him.

The Motivational Gift of Exhortation May Appear Callous:

Because this motivational gift places such emphasis on steps of action they may appear callous or insensitive to the feelings and emotions of others.

Motivational exhorter gifts have difficulties actually relating emotionally to the problems of others. They are practical problem solvers by nature and rarely consider the emotional impact a crisis has on others.

If this is your motivational gift, remember that the emotions of people tend to run high in the midst of a "fiery" trial. Others are more able to receive your steps of action if you present your solution with an attitude of compassion for their pain. Love is always welcome and never fails to bring comfort to those that are suffering.

Exhorters Need to Cultivate Listening Skills:

The natural tendency of the exhorter gift is to talk, not to listen. They tend to frequently interrupt others because of their eagerness to give their opinions or advice. Most exhorter gifts are not even aware of this tendency; however, this is an inherent weakness. If you are a motivational gift of exhortation, you will probably need to address this issue.

Self-discipline and growth are your answers and this problem can be easily corrected through developing a "listening ear." It is always best to listen quietly to others before you offer an opinion. This will probably not seem familiar to you at first, as this is a learned rather than natural attribute; however, the rewards are great.

Tends to be Opinionated:

This motivational gift can be so outspokenly opinionated that they may seem to dismiss all other opinions. This can become fertile ground for the cultivation of contention and conflict in the Body of Christ.

This is an earmark of the gift of exhortation, but this weakness can be tempered by learning to soften the manner in which an opinion is delivered. Also, the opinions of others are important. The gift of exhortation needs to cultivate and convey a respectful attitude concerning the thoughts and opinions of others. A sign of spiritual maturity is the ability to agree to disagree without harming the relationship.

May Appear Overconfident:

The motivational gift of exhortation has the tendency to appear overly self-confident in their "steps of action." Exhorter gifts are normally humble people, surrendered to the Lord, but they are often incorrectly perceived by others as prideful.

The Motivational Gift of Exhortation is Fast Thinking:

This motivational gift has a tendency to come up with solutions while a person is still telling the problem. The rapidity with which the "steps" are given may leave the impression that the person with the problem is secondary to the problem.

The motivational gift of exhortation commonly blurts out their answer without seeming to regard the emotions or feelings of others concerned. Timing is crucial in the art of communication. The answer here is to learn first to be a good listener and to prayerfully seek the counsel of the Holy Spirit; then offer the counsel.

The Motivational Gift of Exhortation in a Ditch:

Any motivational gift not surrendered to the Lord can fall in the ditch. An exhorter gift in this condition has a tendency to become controlling and manipulating. At this point, they can become offended or even angry when their counsel is not received and acted upon.

Some of the Secular Professional Aptitudes This Motivational Gift:

This motivational gift is invaluable to a business as they are intuitive problem solvers. They can hear about a problem and can easily see solutions (or they will seek to find a solution to the problem).

They are excellent in customer relations, as they are able to deal with all types of personalities easily.

Motivational exhorter gifts view a problem as a new opportunity to display their problem solving skills. As a result, they never tire of hearing complaints.

This motivational gift is always promoting the good in things. They promote public relations, progress, excellence, continued growth and maturity.

The gift of exhortation is a blessing in the work place. They have a happy, positive attitude.

Exhorter gifts are not easily dismayed by problems and their demeanor encourages others. They have a calming effect on those around them.

The motivational gift of exhortation is not easily disenchanted by setbacks and they can usually find a bright side to any problem.

The Motivational Gift of Exhortation Especially Excels as:

Advertising Executive   Receptionist
Speech Therapist   Ambassador
Guidance Counselor   Teacher
Recreation Director   Sociologist
Claims Service   Realtor
Special Ed. Teacher   Social Worker
Travel Agent   Music Teacher
Religious Education Director

Motivational Gift of Giving

Chapter 6

The motivational gift of giving is unique in that they spend their life for others. They share with others without even thinking about it. Their giving springs forth from an inherent spiritual yearning to give. This motivational gift seeks places to give and they are sensitive and obedient to the leading of the Holy Spirit in their giving. Motivational givers offer up their gifts as a part of their worship unto the Lord.

The Motivational Gift of Giving is Alert to the Needs of Others:

If this is your motivational gift, you are alert to valid needs that others may overlook. You are easily able to discern a need that may not be obvious. You tend to care deeply about the well-being of others and you are perceptive where unspoken needs are concerned.

Susanna, Joanna, Dorcus

God used godly women to be givers into the ministry of Jesus. **Susanna** and **Joanna** were some of those supporters that God used to meet the needs of Jesus' ministry.

> "and Joanna the wife of Chuza, Herod's steward, and Susanna, and many others who provided for Him from their substance.." Luke 8:3

These women were helping to support them out of their own means.

Dorcus was also a New Testament motivational gift of giving. Giving was her lifestyle.

> "At Joppa there was a certain disciple named Tabitha, which is translated Dorcas. This woman was full of good works and charitable deeds which she did." Acts 9:36

This Gift is Naturally Hospitable:

This motivational gift enjoys people and is very hospitable. They tend to view hospitality as another opportunity to give.

Has a Positive Attitude:

This particular gift normally has a very positive, sunny outlook on life. They are adventurous and they are not afraid to take calculated risks. They are not overly concerned about failure, and if they fail, they are not devastated. They learn from their mistakes and usually simply rebuild.

The Motivational Gift of Giving is Uncomfortable with Accolades:

The motivational gift of giving desires to give quietly to effective ministries and projects. They do not "sound a trumpet" when they give and usually become uncomfortable when singled out or publicly thanked. They have no desire for accolades or credits. Often times, they request that their giving remain anonymous.

This Gift Encourages Others to Give:

Usually, the only time that a motivational giver speaks publicly about their giving is when they are attempting to motivate and encourage others to give also. To them, it could be likened to "priming the pump." The thought is that others will see the need and become motivated to partake in the project.

The Giving Gift Possesses Business Acuity:

An earmark of this motivational gift is they possess seemingly supernatural business abilities. Creative ideas are birthed in them and they have an intuitive sense in how to translate those ideas into financial abundance. God has not only called them to be givers, but has given them the means and ways to accomplish that purpose.

The motivational gift of giving possesses an uncanny sense concerning the business world. This enables them to make wise purchases and investments. They are financial visionaries and perceive opportunities in businesses that others overlook or dismiss.

Is a Hard Worker:

If this is your motivational gift, you are most likely a hard worker and love the challenges that come with being successful in business. You probably tend to be a "workaholic," so this is an area that you would be wise to monitor.

Worships God in Their Giving:

If this is your motivational gift, you will find that your giving is a part of your worship toward the Lord. The act of giving is spiritual to you, and you will often give without being asked. You are sensitive to the Holy Spirit, and you love to give in obedience to the leading of the Holy Spirit. By the same token, you are not quick to give unless prompted by the Lord. Your heart is to follow Him, not emotions.

The Motivational Gift of Giving Heavily Relies on Their Partner:

Unlike most of the motivational gifts, this gift relies heavily on his or her partner in the operation of the gift. The motivational giving gift seeks the counsel and agreement of their partner to confirm the amount of the gift. Unity between the two is an important factor in their giving. Often, the two are delighted to find that they have separately received in their spirits the same gift to give.

When Gifts are an Answer to Prayer:

The motivational gift of giving receives great joy when their gift is an answer to the prayer of another. It is a confirmation to the giver that they have heard correctly from the Lord.

Gifts are of High Quality:

If you are a motivational gift of giving, you will find that it is important to you to give gifts of exceptional quality. You are always concerned that your gifts be of the highest quality possible because your giving is part of your worship before the throne of the Most High God. The desire of your heart is give God your very best.

The Motivational Gift of Giving Connects to the Recipient:

If this is your motivational gift, you will find that you need to feel a connection to the work or person that receives your gift. This is a biblical attitude, as the one who supports a ministry receives the same rewards from the Lord as the one who goes and does the preaching. Every soul saved is accounted to all concerned in each work.

Is Value Minded:

If this is your motivational gift, you probably tend toward frugality and like to get the best value for the money you spend. You recognize and appreciate a bargain. You are gifted in godly business principles, which is why you are so successful.

Possesses Financial Wisdom:

If this is your motivational gift, you are supernaturally equipped with both natural and God-given wisdom concerning finances. You are divinely called and blessed to prosper financially and to bless others as the Lord leads.

Operates With Great Integrity:

The motivational gift of giving usually abides by a rather strict code of ethics. This gift reverences God, and their giving is directly tied to their love and worship of the Lord.

This motivational gift lives to give, and all that they do springs forth from strong character values. It would never occur to them to compromise their business ethics for monetary gain. Dishonesty would cause their profit to be tainted, thereby tainting their gift.

The Motivational Gift of Giving is Philanthropic:

Motivational givers are philanthropic in nature meaning they are benevolent towards others. They possess a kind heart and they are very caring. This motivational gift is easily moved by compassion.

The Motivational Gift of Giving's Area of Expertise:

The motivational gift of giver is called and ordained of God to be successful in business. They are comfortable in dealing with large sums of money. Sometimes others may incorrectly believe that they focus more on temporal values instead of eternal values. This is an unfair assessment. Money never owns a motivational gift of giving. It is important to remember that this is their God given gift and area of expertise.

Heart Attitude of the Motivational Gift of Giving:

A motivational gift of giving needs to closely monitor their heart when giving. The carnal or natural man has a tendency to use money as a means of asserting undue control on others. As long as we are in this earth, each of us must continually deal with our flesh. Therefore, the heart attitude of this motivational gift could easily, almost imperceptibly, shift from "obedience to God" to a "justifiable right to manipulate because of money given."

The solution for the motivational gift of giving is to release every gift to the Lord. If God is the recipient of your gift, you are at liberty. It then becomes the possession of the Lord.

Even if you later become disillusioned with a person or ministry, any gift that has been given to the Lord was

81

received by the Lord. God is still blessed by your giving. He will handle everything else. God keeps a perfect set of books.

Bear in mind that ministries belong to the Lord, not to those who support them. The direction of a ministry must be directed only by God. When a motivational giving gift releases money into a work, he must essentially release it to the Lord and trust God with it. Giving is essentially an act of faith in God.

Wants Others to Give Also:

It is important to remember that the Lord never pressures anyone to give. God looks at the heart motive rather than the size of the gift. Not all are able to give large gifts, but God honors a cheerful giver. Jesus honored the widow's mite, and the same principle holds true today.

The act of giving is very personal to this motivational gift, and is a reflection of the giver's intimate relationship with God.

This Gift Resists Pressure to Give:

The motivational gift of giving balks at being pressured or manipulated. There are times that this seeming lack of response to pressure appeals may appear to be a lack of generosity. It is not! The motivational giver gives freely from the heart, but their act of giving must be led by the Holy Spirit, not their emotions. They resist and resent pressure of any kind.

Is a Good Steward:

Most motivational gifts of giving live a rather frugal lifestyle. Some may take that for selfishness, greed or even fear. However, this motivational gift takes the stewardship of the blessings that they have received from the Lord quite seriously. They are quick to give when they feel led to give. They are not prone to wasting finances.

The Motivational Gift of Giving in the Ditch:

A motivational gift of giving that is not surrendered to the Lord easily goes back into fleshly or carnal attitudes. This motivational gift gone to seed will usually attach "strings" to their giving. At that point they can attempt to control the ministries or persons that have received their financial help. Again, if the gift is always given to the Lord, the heart attitude remains correct.

The motivational gift of giving can easily slide into pride and attempt to control a work or ministry by their financial support. The thought that must always take precedence is that all gifts are given unto the Lord and the Lord cannot be controlled.

Some of the Secular Professional Aptitudes of This Motivational Gift:

- This motivational gift is very entrepreneurial. They can sense when a business will be successful and create wealth. They consistently take calculated risks, and are usually successful in their endeavors.

- The motivational gift of giving is intuitive in business matters. They are well informed and have an extensive comprehension of their field, industry and markets.

- The motivational gift of giver is blessed with a God-given ability to create wealth. You could say "everything he touches turns to gold." The world refers to this as the "Midas touch."

The Motivational Gift of Giving Excels at:

Manager	Banker/Stock Broker
Inventor	Business Teacher
Business Consultant	Wholesaler
Missionary	Manufacturer;
Insurance Agent	Investor
Salesman	Contractor
Advertiser	Business Owner

Motivational Gift of Organization

Chapter 7

"Having then gifts differing according to the grace that is given to us, whether prophecy, let us prophesy according to the proportion of faith; Or ministry, let us wait on our ministering: or he that teacheth, on teaching; Or he that exhorteth, on exhortation: he that giveth, let him do it with simplicity; **he that ruleth, with diligence;** he that sheweth mercy, with cheerfulness." Romans 12:6-8." *KJV*

"he that ruleth, with diligence;" The Greek word "proisteemi" is translated "ruleth" in the KJV of the Bible. It means "to set over; to be over; to superintend; to preside over; to be a protector or guardian; to care for; to give attention to; to give aid."

In our vernacular today, an accurate description would be "he that organizes or administrates." These two terms are interchangeable.

An organizer is a leader; by definition one that stands in front of others. An earmark of this gift is that the organizer is particularly adept at perceiving not only the overall vision, but every minute detail connected to the vision. They are then able to divide the task into smaller segments, and delegate each segment to the specific talents of the available helpers. They are proficient in matching tasks to skills

The Motivational Gift of Organization is a Visionary:

This motivational gift has the ability to first visualize a specific goal, and then to break it down into the logical steps needed to best accomplish that goal.

The motivational gift of organization intuitively captures the overall picture and then clarifies the long-range goal for the team. They "see" what is necessary to make the vision happen. This gift sets about dividing the tasks and assigning or delegating each task to a qualified team leader.

Their organizational skills are layered. They choose a team leader and they expect that leader to build their team to accomplish their assigned task.

Joseph was an excellent example of an organizer. Even as a slave, he brought order to his owner's business affairs. In the jails, his skills quickly brought him into favor. Joseph was destined by God for his position in Egypt. The motivational gift of organization was placed within him at the time of his creation, and it was that gifting that brought him to the fulfillment of his destiny in the Lord. His life can be read in Genesis 37-50 and in each chapter; his gifting can be readily recognized.

Nehemiah was gifted with the motivational gift of organization. He was called of the Lord to rebuild the walls of Jerusalem and his organizational gifting is clearly recognizable in the book of Nehemiah.

Jethro, the father-in-law of Moses, laid before Moses a plan to organize others to hear and judge the people. Jethro's layered organizational skills lightened the burden for Moses and brought a system of order to the task of caring for the people. This is found in Exodus 18:17-23

The Organizational Gift is Neat and Organized Personally:

This motivational gift abhors disorganization. They are compelled to organize and bring order in every area of their life, both personal and professional.

The motivational organizer gift has an intense desire to complete tasks as quickly as possible. They lay out the work in a practical time efficient manner. If possible, they tend to work until it is finished.

Is a Natural Delegator:

The ability to delegate tasks to others is a major facet of this motivational gift. They are proficient at delegating a task to just the right person. The organizing gift comprehends the talents and limitations of those around them. They are aware of who would be a perfect fit for a specific task. They tend to help develop the talents of others and part of their gifting is that they bring out the best in others.

The ability to successfully delegate tasks is one of the most instrumental roles of the organizer. They are equipped with phenomenal insight in delegating responsibilities and fitting the correct person for each task.

The organizer gift also knows what can and cannot be delegated to another. This motivational gift has the capacity to lead and to build leadership qualities in others. The tasks they delegate to others are measured carefully to ensure success.

Friction may arise periodically as there are times that delegating the responsibilities may be perceived by others as an unwillingness to do the job personally. This is an incorrect assessment on the part of others, as the talent of being able to successfully delegate tasks is an earmark of this motivational gift.

The solution to this misunderstanding is to learn to verbally communicate well. The workers need to catch the vision of the organizer (administrator) and "see" their part in bringing the entire picture to fruition. This is only accomplished successfully through skilled detailed communication.

Deeply Respects Legitimate Authority:

This motivational gift has a tendency to stand on sidelines until he or she is given the authority to lead. They are able to follow instructions as well as give instructions. They have well defined boundaries that they do not cross.

The organizer will usually assume responsibility if there is no structured leadership in command.

This Gift Is Able to Endure Criticism

This motivational gift is willing to endure negative reactions from others in order to accomplish the fulfillment of the task. Emotionally, they are able to continue working towards the goal in spite of criticism or disagreement. They are able to make tough decisions and assume full responsibility for those decisions. The gift of organization does not shirk from responsibility or accountability.

Often this willingness of an organizer or administrator to endure negative reaction is mistakenly taken as callousness toward the feelings or opinions of others. Again, the solution to this problem lies in open communication. The organizer must make him or herself available to their people. Many negative reactions can be avoided if the delegates have confidence that the organizer is there for their questions and directions.

Also, it is never possible to please all the people all the time. One of the strengths of the gift of organization is that they realize that people are different and have different points of view. Diplomacy and tact are able to render a firm decision with an attitude of love.

The Motivational Gift of Organization Must Impart the Vision:

If you are a motivational gift of organization, it is critical to the unity of the team that you impart your vision and plan of action in detail. Clarity helps to bring cohesiveness to your team. Effective communication is not the strongest attribute of this gift. The organizer gift needs to focus on developing communication skills.

If this is your gift, you may have the tendency to neglect to explain why tasks must be done in a certain manner. This often makes people feel misused. Articulate verbal communication solves this problem. Learn to "over communicate."

Enjoys Challenges:

The motivational gift of organization receives great pleasure in seeing others come together to rejoice over a completed task. A job well done brings a sense of tremendous satisfaction.

This motivational gift desires to move on to a new challenge when a previous task is completed satisfactorily.

They must have a new horizon, a new challenge, a new mountain to climb. They are motivated to work hard and to find solutions.

This Gift is a Prolific Note Writer:

Another earmark of this motivational gift is that they constantly write notes to themselves. If you are an organizing gift, you probably have little yellow sticky notes everywhere, even on your Day Planner.

Hates Routine Tasks:

The motivational gift of organization does not enjoy doing mundane, routine tasks. It is the challenge that feeds their creativity and motivates them. They normally assign the routine maintenance of the completed work to others.

Is a Hard Worker:

This gift is a hard worker and is driven to complete tasks in an efficient manner as swiftly as possible. It is difficult for the organizer to find a "stopping place," and they tend to work long, arduous hours without regard to the limitations of their team.

If this is your gift, your "drive" can easily give rise to grumbling among your team members. They may correctly feel that you are insensitive to their other responsibilities, as you tend to focus on the project rather than the people involved in the project. Your attention tends to be so focused on the task at hand, that the needs of the people working under you may not even come to mind. You probably need to become more attuned to the people on your team.

The Organizer Tends to Views People as Resources:

If you are an organizer, you most likely have a tendency to view others as your resources. This often causes those working with you to feel that the project is your greatest priority and that your team members are secondary.

Unfortunately that assessment is often valid as an organizer easily becomes so focused on the task at hand that they tend to forget to take into account the individual persons that they have involved in the task. If this is your gift, you probably need to evaluate this issue periodically. It is an unintentional misstep, but it can cause wounded feelings in others and no vision ever comes to fruition without the personal involvement of a team. Teams are made up of people and happy teams are productive teams.

The Motivational Gift of Organization Needs to Develop People Skills:

Your tremendous God given abilities in organizational skills is inherent within you; however, people skills tend to be a learning experience. This is a major weak area for you.

A demanding, pushy boss is most likely a motivational gift of organization that is not surrendered to the Lord. The natural talents are there, just not submitted to the leading of the Holy Spirit. As the precious Holy Spirit grows and matures the fruit of the Spirit within this gift, unity prevails and the tasks are completed in a peaceful work setting.

The Motivational Gift of Organization and the Family Needs:

This motivational gift naturally tends to drive his or her self to complete the project "no matter what the cost" and it often results in the neglect of their personal or family needs.

The fruit of temperance helps here. This motivational gift can easily fall into a routine of overworking and even bringing their work home with them. Personal priorities must be defined and enforced in order to sustain a healthy lifestyle balance. It is important that the motivational gift of organization establish and maintain personal boundaries balancing their work and family time.

This Gift and Home Responsibilities:

The organizer gift often neglects routine home responsibilities due to their intense interest in the "job." They may even become critical of others that are not willing to sacrifice their personal life for the task. Again, establishing and maintaining personal boundaries that bring a balance to their work and home life is the solution.

Areas of Concern:

The motivational gift of organization has three areas that they need to closely monitor. The first is they have a tendency to become so engrossed in the project that they tend to forget the individuals who are working under them. This can cause resentment and even offense in their workers. The compensation for this would be to work at developing an alertness concerning the people under them. It is also helpful to appreciate and acknowledge the contributions that others bring to the table. This gift leads, and the leader should be available to those that work under them. It helps when the organizer will "hear" and consider what their co-workers are saying.

The second is the motivational gift of organization has a tendency to be a workaholic. Care should be taken to separate work and home life, not only for the organizer, but also for the individuals on the teams that work with them.

The third is the organizational gift has a tendency to "get lost" in the task. It can become all absorbing to them as they tend to "tunnel vision." This can cause a negative "ripple" effect in their personal relationships. If this is your motivational gift, this is an area that you should closely monitor.

The Motivational Gift of Organization in a Ditch:

This motivational gift in a ditch can become difficult, controlling and at times, even sharp in their mannerisms with others. When not surrendered to the Lord, this gift has a tendency to "micro-manage" both the task at hands and the lives of the people working under them. Intimacy with the Lord is their answer addresses this weakness. Walking in the love of God is a lifestyle that brings peace. Peace within creates peace without.

Some of the Secular Professional Aptitudes of This Motivational Gift:

- The motivational gift of organization is a leader. They excel as managers, supervisors, directors and committee heads. All of these positions require teams of people working under an organizer to complete a job.

- This motivational gift is able to devise methods and procedures that work and they will quickly scrap any procedure that is ineffective.

- The organizer is a "get it done" type of a person.

- The organizer gift is adept at delegating tasks. They oversee without having a need to do everything themselves. They lead the team.

- When no one is in control, this motivational gift immediately takes charge and begins to develop a workable plan to complete a job or bring the vision into manifestation.

- The motivational gift of organization loves long-range goals and the challenges that are presented with those goals. Short range goals are of little interest to them.

- The organizer gift needs a secretary (or server) because they hate routine tasks. They see the larger picture and are not interested in maintenance or mundane tasks. They are; however, quick to spot even the smallest detail and assign it to a team. Nothing escapes them.

- They are always writing notes, lists and outlines.

- No task is beyond the capabilities of an organizer. They can organize and administrate complex tasks which seem impossible to others.

- The organizer gift is uncomfortable with clutter. They function best in a neat, clean environment. Their offices and homes are clean and organized.

The Motivational Gift of Organization Excels as:

Advertising Executive
Air Traffic controller
Producer
Business Owner
Judge
Reporter
Ambassador
Conductor of Music
Religious Ed. Director
College Professor
Travel Agent
City Planner
Military Officer
Insurance Agent

Radio/TV Manager
Personnel Manager
Recreation Director
Office Manager
Restaurant Manager
Politician
Theologian
School Administrator
Lawyer
Film Director
Store Manager
General Contractor
Marketing Executive

Motivational Gift of Mercy

Chapter 8

The motivational gift of mercy is kind, gentle and compassionate. They are happy to show mercy, and they are quick to help in times of need. Jesus is our best example of mercy.

> "And Jesus, when he came out, saw much people, and was moved with compassion toward them, because they were as sheep not having a shepherd: and he began to teach them many things." Mark 6:34

As for the motivational gift of mercy, they are literally "moved with compassion." The mercy gift is like the leaf that falls into a river and is "borne along" by the rushing waters. They are easily touched by the lives of others and they are "borne along" or "caught up" with the hurts of others. Their heart desire is "rush in" and comfort the hurting. They act quickly, without thought of self and render kindness and encouragement to one in distress.

Jeremiah is true biblical example of a motivational gift of mercy. He had the calling of a prophet, but was so easily touched with the heartache of his people, he was labeled the "weeping prophet." The book of Jeremiah paints an accurate picture of mercy in action.

Joseph, the earthly father of Jesus, was a motivational gift of mercy. Joseph showed tremendous mercy in his reaction when Mary revealed that she was with child. In that day and time, he not only would have been justified in making her a public example, but he most likely faced retribution for his kindness toward her. He married Mary after the angel of God spoke to him, but even before that, he was protective and forgiving of Mary.

"Now the birth of Jesus Christ was as follows: After His mother Mary was betrothed to Joseph, before they came together, she was found with child of the Holy Spirit. Then Joseph her husband, being a just man, and not wanting to make her a public example, was minded to put her away secretly." Matthew 1:18-19

The Motivational Gift of Mercy "Feels" the Atmosphere:

An earmark of the motivational gift of mercy is that they possess the uncanny ability to "feel" or "sense" the atmosphere in an individual or group. They are very intuitive and easily pick up on the emotions of others around them.

This Gift is Attracted to Hurting People:

This motivational gift is drawn to those in distress. It is almost as if they attract the hurting. They have a deep understanding of people in trouble and instinctively move toward them to render help.

Note: Because the motivational mercy gift is strongly attracted to the hurting, their desire to help is often mistaken for an interest in the opposite sex. This can present real problems and is a pit fall that the mercy gift often encounters and must take care to avoid when ministering to the opposite sex.

People who are hurting easily transfer their affections to the one who is helping them. Motivational mercy gifts need to exercise great caution. The wisdom of God would be to minister care to those of the same sex. Where the opposite sex is concerned, it is best to counsel them in the presence of another, or ask a member of the same sex to meet with the one that is hurting.

The Motivational Gift of Mercy Desires to Remove Hurts:

The motivational mercy gift experiences an intense desire to remove hurts from the lives of others. This can lead to the mercy gift unconsciously assuming responsibility for the life of another and result in an emotional overload. This motivational gift must remember that it is God alone that heals the broken hearted.

The Mercy Gift Sees Beyond the Physical:

The motivational gift of server focuses mainly on the practical, physical needs of others while the motivational gift of mercy is especially gifted in sensing the unseen needs of others in the emotional and mental realms.

This motivational gift possesses a keen sensitivity for the mental and emotional distress of others. The mercy gift literally experiences the pain of another. In the presence of grief, they truly grieve. They pick up on (and feel the impact of) the emotions that emanate from those around them.

Their natural empathy with the emotional feelings of those around them may cause others to believe they are led by emotions and not reason. This motivational gift is finely tuned to the Holy Spirit and may often appear to be unrealistic. While their emotions play a huge part in who they are, they are quick to follow the leading of the Spirit.

This Gift Tends to Rescue Others:

The motivational gift of mercy can enable a dysfunctional person by becoming too involved emotionally. This does not usually last long as they soon realize there is no positive change in the person they are helping. As this motivational gift matures in the Lord, they are more balanced in their approach to helping others.

Because of their great tenderness and gentleness, this motivational gift can fall into the habit of "rescuing" others instead of actually helping. The mercy gift must exercise more caution than the other gifts and be led of the Holy Spirit instead of their emotions.

Ministering to the emotional or mental realm of another is never "cut and dried." Only when you are completely dependent on the Holy Spirit to guide you can you be truly used of the Lord in this area.

The Motivational Gift of Mercy May Appear Indecisive:

The mercy gift may often appear indecisive. They have a desire to always be fair and not wound another. They tend to "second guess" themselves and are often accused of "waffling" by others.

They actually weigh all known facts prayerfully and carefully before making decisions concerning others. This gift is however, able to make and adhere to decisions. Their strength is not obvious. They are "velvet covered steel."

This Gift Has Need of Firm Godly Boundaries:

If you are a motivational gift of mercy, you will probably find that it is difficult for you to be firm with someone that is in emotional distress or pain; however, many times a loving firmness is what is needed. There are situations where "tough love" is the only true solution.

You also tend to be uncomfortable with, and dislike confrontation or conflict. As a result, you most likely find it unpleasant to say, "No" to a request from someone that is distressed.

Boundaries are not inherent in your nature if you are a motivational gift of mercy, so learning to establish and enforce godly boundaries is probably difficult for you. You must learn anyway. Boundaries are borders and bring godly order into your life. There is no possible way for anyone to live in the peace of God without godly boundaries.

Chooses Words Carefully:

This motivational gift is finely tuned to and deeply cares about the well-being of others. They are keenly aware of words and actions that can bring pain to another.

Because the mercy gift is so sensitive to words and actions that cause hurt, that very sensitivity is often misconstrued as defending another's offense.

The motivational gift of mercy often attempts to "tone down" words of reprimand or criticism. At times they may appear to defend vigorously; however, their true motive is to speak the truth with great love. Their presentation is with great mercy applied. They tend to choose their words carefully.

The mercy gift is kind and always considers the feelings of others. Even when treated despitefully, this gift is reluctant to speak unkindly and they have no thought of retaliation.

Instinctively Discerns the Motives of Others:

The mercy gift is able to discern the true motives of others. Many times they appear to be idealistic and naïve; in reality, they are realistic and longsuffering.

There is neither guile nor deception in the motivational mercy gift. They are pure of heart and prefer to think the best of others.

The Motivational Gift of Mercy is a Committed Friend:

The motivational gift of mercy is hard to get to know on a personal intimate level. They have strong walls of defense around them; however once they let you in, they become a committed friend for life.

Their close friends tend to be likeminded and also exhibit a keen sensitivity to the needs of others.

"How can two walk together except they be agreed?" Amos 3: 3

This motivational gift is drawn to those that possess a tender spirit and a pure heart.

If this is your motivational gift, you tend to quickly close your spirit off to those who are insincere or callous to others. You operate with great gentleness and kindness and you probably feel personally wounded when you see someone treat another roughly or be harsh in their mannerisms toward them.

Ruth was a motivational gift of mercy. The entire Book of Ruth reveals her kind and gentle nature. Her faithfulness and honor are noteworthy. Her story is a study into a mercy gift.

This Gift is Naturally Trusting on a Surface Level:

The motivational gift of mercy is naturally trusting on a basic level as they assume the best in others. However; intimate, deep personal trust is cultivated over time with the gift of mercy. This motivational gift tends to be positive and uplifting,

They are also trustworthy. Faithfulness is an integral part of their personality. It would never occur to them to betray a trust.

The Motivational Gift of Mercy Experiences the Emotions of Others:

This gift experiences pure joy when they see others blessed and they grieve deeply when they see others hurt. They sincerely, deeply care about others.

Some of the Secular Professional Aptitudes of This Motivational Gift:

- The mercy gift is very creative and artistic. They are excellent as interior decorators. They are able to visualize a project and then implement that vision.

- This motivational gift is gentle, kind, considerate and therefore easy to get along with. They are peacemakers and mediators.

- The mercy gift is usually happy, cheerful and upbeat. Most people enjoy working with them.

- The motivational gift of mercy is able to sense dissension. They will take it upon themselves to attempt to talk a person out of anger and hurt. They bring a balance to the workplace.

- This motivational gift is an excellent diplomat. They are good at public relations, client relations, and liaisons between the company and its suppliers. They are natural peacemakers.

- The mercy gift does not find it easy to make a business decision. They are a part of the team, but not usually the leader of the team.

- This motivational gift is more interested in building relationships than in the projects at hand. They are "people persons." Relationships are their primary focus.

- They are more interested in the welfare of clients or employees than in the job. The people involved take precedence over the task or achieving the goal.

The Motivational Gift of Mercy Excels as:

Caregiver	Artist
Composer	Veterinarian
Art Teacher	Nurse

Florist
Conservationist
Fashion Designer
Interior Decorator
Nutritionist

Writer/Poet
Nanny
Musician
Song Writer

Personal Gift Profile

Chapter 9

This profile is designed to help you to locate the gift God placed in you. There are a series of questions that are inherent in each gift. Choose the answers that best fit you.

The questions are to be answered and scored with:

Never	value 0
Rarely	value 1
Sometimes	value 2
Usually	value 3
Often	value 4
Always	value 5

The Gift of Prophecy:

Strong Traits:

Very intuitive in your perceptions	_____
Sees things black or white	_____
Consistently confronts sin	_____
Needs to see fruit of repentance	_____
Strict concerning accountability	_____
Easily empathizes with others	_____
Perseveres; never quits	_____
Never plays political games	_____
Consistently glorifies God	_____
Life is strictly Word based	_____
Consistently demands excellence	_____
Does not easily make friends	_____
Is an effective communicator	_____

Speaks boldly and frankly   _____
Adheres to a strict ethical code   _____
             Total score   _____

Weaknesses:
Tendency to be harsh   _____
Tendency to be judgmental   _____
Tendency to be sharp or critical   _____
Tendency to correct others   _____
Can be controlling   _____
             Total score   _____

The Gift of Serving

Strong Traits:
Very practical personality   _____
Quickly spots practical needs   _____
Enjoys manual projects/jobs   _____
Rate serving others as primary thing   _____
Demonstrate your love by serving   _____
Serves without being told   _____
Detail oriented   _____
Naturally hospitable   _____
Hard worker   _____
Hates time limits on jobs   _____
Possesses organizational skills   _____
Finds it difficult to say "No"   _____
May clash with bureaucracy   _____
Easily sidetracked to another job   _____
Needs the appreciation of others   _____
             Total score   _____

Weaknesses:
Serves to validate their value   _____

Tendency to become bossy _____
Tendency to become controlling _____
Easily offended _____
Complains to others _____
Total score _____

The Gift of Teaching

Strong Traits:
Is intellectual _____
Is a Prolific reader _____
Is an avid researcher _____
Is systematic in presentation _____
Always validates new truths _____
Believes their gift is primary _____
Easily sidetracked to new topic _____
Research first love _____
Teaching second love _____
Critiques other teachers _____
Difficulty receiving from others _____
Not afraid of controversy _____
Uses established references _____
Uses Biblical examples _____
Sharp mental acuity _____
Total score _____

Weaknesses:
Easily falls into intellectual pride _____
Can be harsh, arrogant, abrasive _____
Forgets to factor in the Holy Spirit _____
Does not receive correction easily _____
Can become legalistic _____
Total score _____

The Motivational Gift of Exhortation

Strong Traits:

Is a "people person" _____
Looks for the blessings in trials _____
Only sees victory _____
Very practical _____
Needs to hear practical application _____
Delights in helping others _____
Not competitive by nature _____
Non-judgmental personality _____
Needs to see "fruit of their work" _____
Interacts well with others _____
Empathizes "steps of action" _____
Is a problem solver _____
Is a worshipper of the Lord _____
Is a living witness for God _____
Is a fast thinker _____
Has a happy, positive attitude _____
Not easily discouraged _____
Total Score _____

Weaknesses:

Can be easily offended _____
May use manipulation _____
May attempt to control others _____
Total Score _____

The Motivational Gift of Giving

Strong Traits:

Acutely alert to the needs of others _____
Naturally hospitable _____
Has a positive attitude _____

Is uncomfortable with accolades _____
Encourages others to give _____
Possesses intuitive business acuity _____
Is a hard worker _____
Worships God in their giving _____
Relies heavily on their partner _____
Gifts are of high quality _____
Is value minded _____
Operates with great integrity _____
Happy when gifts are answer to prayer _____
Has financial wisdom _____
Resists pressure to give _____
              Total score _____

Weaknesses:
May use money to control others _____
Feels others "owe" for the gift _____
Attaches strings to their giving _____
Easily slides into pride _____
Feels they own recipient of gift _____
              Total Score _____

Motivational Gift of Organization

Strong Traits:
Is a visionary _____
Is neat and organized personally _____
Is a natural delegator _____
Respects legitimate authority _____
Is able to endure criticism _____
Enjoys challenges _____
Is a prolific note writer _____
Hates routine tasks _____
Is a hard worker _____

Enjoys long range goals _____
Hates short range goals _____
Is a natural leader _____
Is able to organize difficult tasks _____
Possesses tremendous "drive" _____
                    Total Score _____

Weaknesses:
Tends to be a "workaholic" _____
Neglects family for the job _____
Does not communicate clearly _____
Does not impart the vision well _____
Views people as "resources _____
Lacks "people skills" _____
                    Total score _____

Motivational Gift of Mercy

Strong Traits:
Naturally kind and gentle nature _____
Easily "feels" the emotions of others _____
Attracted to hurting people _____
Intense desire to remove hurts _____
"Sees" beyond the physical _____
May appear indecisive _____
Chooses words carefully _____
Discerns the motives of others _____
Is a committed friend _____
Experiences the emotions of others _____
Naturally compassionate _____
Possesses a pure heart _____
Trustworthy _____
Strong ethical nature _____
Hard to get to know intimately _____

Total score   _____

Weaknesses:
Enables others to be victims   _____
Doesn't say "No" when needed   _____
Snared with the problems of others   _____
Easily manipulated emotionally   _____
Easily "used" by others   _____
                    Total score   _____

Scoring

Add both scores together for each gift. When finished adding the scores for each gift, you will discover your gift. Your highest score is your primary gifting. Your second highest score is your secondary gifting.

Made in the USA
Monee, IL
05 August 2020